Revision Notes
for
Higher
Chemistry

D A Buchanan
(Moray House School of Education,
University of Edinburgh)

J R Melrose
(formerly Lenzie Academy)

Published by
Chemcord
Inch Keith
East Kilbride
Glasgow

ISBN 9781870570954

© Buchanan and Melrose, 2014

Printed by Bell and Bain Ltd, Glasgow

Note to students

The course

- This book is designed to cover all of the essential content of the CfE Higher Chemistry Course.
- Information that may be of use to you can be found in the Data Booklet. A copy of the Data Booklet can be downloaded from the SQA website:
  (http://www.sqa.org.uk/files_ccc/ChemistryDataBookletSQPH.pdf)

Your revision

- You are more likely to benefit from your revision if you work at a steady rate and have a study plan.
- You can indicate your knowledge and understanding of each statement with a ✓ in the □ at the left hand side.
- You can also mark statements with a highlighter pen.
- If there is some part of the course that you do **not** understand, ask your teacher.
- A lot of calculations in the Higher Chemistry course involve simple proportion. In this book the symbol ' ←——→ ' shows that a calculation involves proportion.
  Check with your mathematics or chemistry teacher if you are unsure of the layout used.
- Key formulae (relationships) are given on page 4 of the Data Booklet.
- The tests in "***Assessment Tests for Higher Chemistry***" will check that you have mastered the various parts of a topic and help you pin-point areas of difficulty.
- You can practise examination-type questions using "***Revision Questions for Higher Chemistry***". This is a useful way of checking that you have really understood the topic and can apply your knowledge and problem solving skills.

Index

Chemical Changes and Structure

Nature's Chemistry

Chemistry in Society

Unit 1   Chemical Changes and Structure

1. CONTROLLING THE RATE

Factors that affect reaction rate (revision)

☐ For a chemical reaction to take place, reactant particles must collide with each other.

(a) Particle size/surface area

☐ The rate of a chemical reaction increases as the particle size of a reactant decreases (surface area increases).

☐ The new surfaces give more opportunities for collisions between reactant particles.

solid particle   cut into two pieces   new surfaces exposed; more opportunities for collisions

(b) Concentration (or pressure)

☐ The rate of a chemical reaction decreases as the concentration of a reactant decreases.

☐ As concentration decreases, there are fewer opportunities for collisions.

high concentration of reactants   low concentration of reactants

☐ With gases, pressure is a measure of the concentration. The rate of industrial reactions involving gases is increased by increasing the pressure of the reactants.

(c) Temperature

The rate of a chemical reaction increases as the temperature of the reactants increases.

Successful collisions

(a) Activation energy

☐ Molecules are constantly colliding without a reaction taking place. This is because not all collisions between reactant particles result in the formation of product,

> *e.g. nitrogen and oxygen molecules are constantly colliding in the air without a reaction taking place.*

☐ For a chemical reaction to occur, reactant particles must collide with sufficient energy to result in a **successful collision**. This is the basis for the collision theory.

☐ Energy is required to break all bonds in the reactant molecules before new bonds can be formed.

Example: The reaction of hydrogen with oxygen

energy needed to break bonds
before new bonds can be formed

☐ The **activation energy (E$_A$)** is the minimum kinetic energy required to break the bonds in colliding particles, i.e. for successful collisions to take place and for a reaction to occur.

☐ The rate of a reaction that has a high activation energy can be increased if energy is supplied to increase the number of particles with energy greater than the activation energy.

(b) Collision geometry

☐ In addition to having the necessary activation energy, particles must have the correct collision geometry for some reactions to occur.

Example: **The reaction of carbon monoxide with nitrogen dioxide**

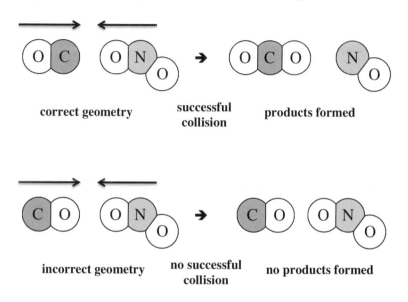

correct geometry   successful collision   products formed

incorrect geometry   no successful collision   no products formed

The effect of temperature on reaction rate

☐ The increase in reaction rate with increasing temperature cannot just be explained on the basis of an increase in the rate of collisions.

☐ Temperature is a measure of the average kinetic energy of the particles in a substance. If the temperature of a substance at T_1 is increased to T_2 then more particles will have energies that are equal to or higher than the activation energy, E_A.

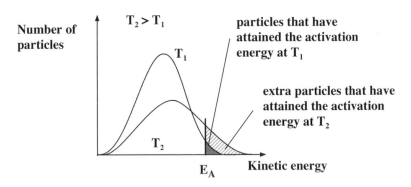

☐ The effect of temperature on reaction rate can be explained in terms of an increase in the number of successful collisions due to an increase in the number of particles with energy greater than the activation energy.

☐ It is possible at low temperatures for no particles to have the activation energy and then no reaction occurs.

☐ A small rise in temperature can cause a large increase in the number of particles having the activation energy and so can result in a large increase in reaction rate,

e.g. *for some reactions the reaction rate doubles for every temperature rise of 10 °C.*

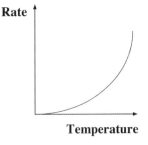

☐ Although most chemical reactions follow this pattern, there are other possibilities.

An explosive reaction

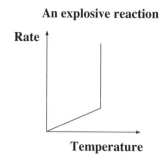

An enzyme reaction

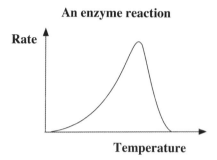

Exothermic and endothermic reactions

☐ An **exothermic** reaction releases energy, usually in the form of heat, to the surroundings. There is a temperature rise since the surroundings takes in (absorbs) the energy produced by the reaction.

☐ The surroundings include the container in which the reaction takes place, the air round about and the reaction mixture itself.

☐ A reaction in which energy is taken in (absorbed) from the surroundings is called an **endothermic** reaction. If heat energy is taken from the surroundings, there is a temperature fall.

☐ With industrial reactions, costs can be incurred in supplying heat energy in order to maintain the rate when the reaction is endothermic.

☐ With exothermic reactions, the energy released can be used to raise the temperature of reactants and reduce costs (see 'The design of an industrial process', page 94). In some cases the heat produced may need to be removed to prevent a 'runaway reaction'.

Bond breaking and bond making

☐ A chemical reaction can be regarded as a series of bond breaking and bond making steps.

Example: The reaction of methane with oxygen (burning of methane)

☐ The activation energy is required to break the bonds in the reactant molecules but energy is released as new bonds in the product molecules are made.

☐ If the total energy change for the bond breaking steps is less than that for the bond making steps, the overall reaction will be **exothermic**. If the total energy for the bond breaking steps is greater than that for the bond making steps, the overall reaction is **endothermic**.

energy for bond breaking < energy for bond making		EXOTHERMIC
energy for bond breaking > energy for bond making		ENDOTHERMIC
(energy in)	(energy out)	

Enthalpy

☐ Every substance contains energy and its energy content is known as its **enthalpy (H)**.

☐ Enthalpy varies from substance to substance and so during a chemical reaction there is an **enthalpy change (ΔH)**.

☐ The enthalpy change is the difference in enthalpy between the products and the reactants; this may be expressed as: $\Delta H = H_P - H_R$ where H_P and H_R are the enthalpies of the products and of the reactants respectively.

☐ While it is impossible to measure absolute enthalpies, it is possible to measure enthalpy changes, i.e. ΔH can be measured but not H_P or H_R.

☐ Enthalpy changes are usually quoted in kilojoules per mole of a reactant or per mole of a product, i.e. $kJ\ mol^{-1}$.

☐ In an exothermic reaction the energy content of the product(s) is less than the energy content of the reactant(s), consequently the sign of ΔH is negative, i.e. $H_P - H_R$ is negative.

In an endothermic reaction the energy content of the product(s) is greater than the energy content of the reactant(s), consequently the sign of ΔH is positive, i.e. $H_P - H_R$ is positive.

Potential energy diagrams

☐ A potential energy diagram can be used to show the energy pathway for a reaction.

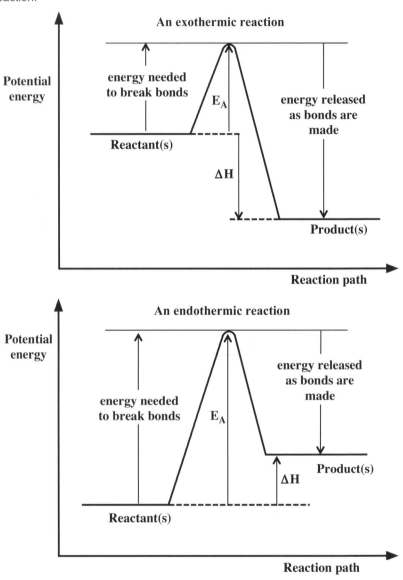

Chemical Changes and Structure

☐ The 'intermediate' that is formed between the reactants and the products at the top of the activation energy barrier is called the **activated complex** and because of its high energy it is very unstable.

Example: The decomposition of a diatomic molecule XY into its elements

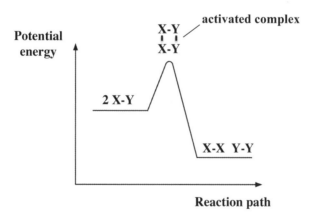

reactants   **activated complex**   **products**

☐ The complex will lose energy and can break up to reform the reactants or break up to form products.

☐ Activation energies and enthalpy changes for reversible reactions can be found from potential diagrams.

Example 1:   The forward reaction is exothermic.

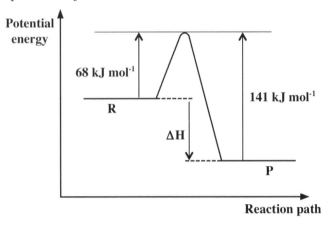

E_A (forward) = **68 kJ mol⁻¹**; E_A (reverse) = **141 kJ mol⁻¹**
ΔH (forward) = **-73 kJ mol⁻¹** (the sign for the enthalpy change is negative)

Example 2:   The forward reaction is endothermic.

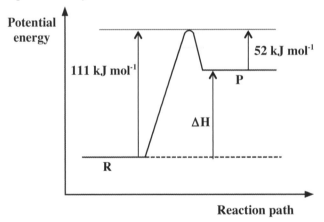

E_A (forward) = **111 kJ mol⁻¹**; E_A (reverse) = **52 kJ mol⁻¹**
ΔH (forward) = **+59 kJ mol⁻¹** (the sign for the enthalpy change is positive)

Catalysts

☐ A **catalyst** speeds up a reaction by decreasing the activation energy. More particles will have an energy equal to or in excess of the lower activation energy. This leads to an increase in the rate of successful collisions and hence reaction rate.

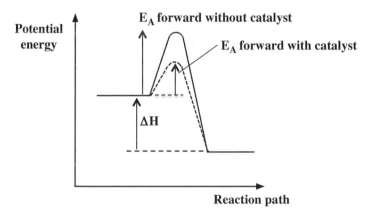

☐ A catalyst also decreases the activation energy for the reverse reaction.

☐ The enthalpy change for a reaction, ΔH, is **not** altered by the use of a catalyst.

2. PERIODICITY

The arrangement of elements in the Periodic Table (revision)

☐ The modern Periodic Table is based on the work of Mendeleev who arranged the known elements in order of increasing atomic weight but he also produced columns by placing elements with similar chemical properties the one below the other.

☐ In order not to destroy the pattern, gaps were left for elements yet to be discovered. He made predictions about the physical properties and chemical behaviour of such elements,

   e.g. he correctly predicted the properties of the element germanium, an element he called eka-silicon.

☐ The Periodic Table allows chemists to make accurate predictions of physical properties and chemical behaviour for any element based on its position.

☐ In the modern Periodic Table elements are arranged in order of increasing atomic number. This reflects the difference in the number of protons in the nucleus of successive elements.

☐ From left to right across a period, there is an increase in the number of outer electrons in atoms of the elements.

☐ Elements in the same group (vertical column) have similar chemical properties resulting from the same number of electrons in the outer shell (energy level) of the atoms.

☐ Atoms of the alkali metals have one electron in the outer shell. The halogen atoms have seven electrons in the outer shell. The noble gas atoms all have a filled outer shell.

☐ Metals are to the left of the Periodic Table and non-metals are to the right. From left to right across the Periodic Table there is a move from metallic to non-metallic characteristics.

☐ The transition metals lie between Group 2 and Group 3.

☐ Most of the gaseous elements are found clustered in the top-right corner of the Periodic Table.

Bonding and structure in the first twenty elements

☐ Differences in electrical conductivity and melting points enable the elements to be grouped according to bonding and structure.

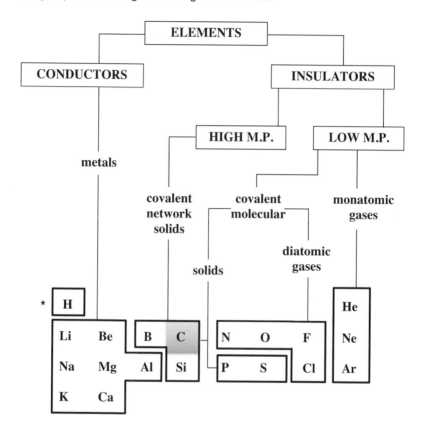

☐ * Hydrogen is a (covalent molecular) diatomic gas.

☐ Carbon has two different covalent network structures, diamond and graphite (see page 15).

☐ Carbon also has different covalent molecular structures called fullerenes (see page 16).

(a) Metals

☐ In metal atoms, the electrons in the outer electron shells are **delocalised**, i.e. not held to a particular atom.

☐ A metallic structure can be thought of as a giant three-dimensional arrangement (known as a **lattice**) of positively charged 'ions' in a pool of detached electrons that are free to move throughout the metal lattice. Each positively charged 'ion' is attracted to the pool of negative electrons and vice versa. These electrostatic attractions constitute the **metallic bonds**. The metallic bonds hold the entire metal lattice together as a single unit.

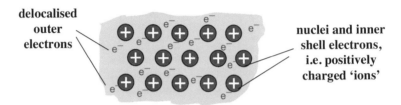

☐ Since the outermost electrons are free to move, metals are good conductors of electricity as both solids and liquids.

☐ A lot of energy is required to overcome the forces of attraction. As a result, metallic bonds are strong (80 - 600 kJ mol⁻¹).

☐ The greater the number of delocalised electrons and consequently the greater the charge on the 'ions', the stronger will be the metallic bond,

e.g. *Group 1 metals have weaker metallic bonds than the corresponding Group 2 metals.*

(b) Covalent network solids

☐ A covalent network structure consists of a giant lattice of covalently bonded atoms. These elements have very high melting points because melting involves breaking of strong covalent bonds.

☐ Boron has a covalent network structure based on interlocking B_{12} molecular units.

☐ Carbon exists in two different crystalline forms, diamond and graphite.

(i) Diamond

In diamond, each carbon atom is at the centre of a regular tetrahedron and surrounded by four other carbon atoms at the corners of the tetrahedron. Each atom forms four covalent bonds by sharing electrons with each of its four nearest neighbours.

Since all the electrons are localised in the covalent bonds, diamond does not conduct electricity. The rigid three dimensional structure with its strong covalent bonds makes diamond very hard and it is used for cutting.

(ii) Graphite

In graphite, each carbon atom forms covalent bonds with three neighbouring atoms. The carbon atoms join to make up a planar arrangement of hexagonal plates which are held together by weak forces of attraction and so easily slip over each other.

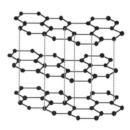

Graphite can be used as a lubricant and as 'lead' in pencils. Unlike diamond (and the fullerenes), graphite is a conductor of electricity. Since only three electrons from each carbon atom are localised through covalent bonding, the fourth electron is free to move.

☐ Silicon has a similar crystal structure to diamond but whereas diamond is a non-conductor of electricity silicon is a semi-conductor.

(c) Covalent molecular solids and gases

☐ A covalent molecular structure consists of discrete (separate) molecules held together by weak intermolecular forces. The typically low melting and boiling points are a result of the weak forces of attraction between the molecules. These forces, known as London dispersion forces, are a type of van der Waals' force (see 'Intermolecular forces', page 26).

☐ Phosphorus and sulphur are solids at room temperature due to their higher molecular masses.

Group 5	diatomic	$N{\equiv}N$
	P_4 tetrahedra	
Group 6	diatomic	$O{=}O$
	S_8 puckered ring	
Group 7	diatomic	$F{-}F$
	diatomic	$Cl{-}Cl$

☐ **Fullerenes** are covalent molecular forms of carbon. The first molecule to be discovered consists of 60 carbon atoms, C_{60}. The pattern of the structure is spherical, similar to a football but considerably smaller.

(d) Monatomic gases

☐ Each of the noble gases consists of atoms with filled outer energy levels and so the atoms are relatively unreactive.

☐ These elements have low melting and boiling points due to the weak intermolecular forces between the atoms.

Trends in the Periodic Table

(a) Physical properties

☐ There are variations in the densities, melting points and boiling points of the elements across a period and down a group.

(b) Covalent radius

☐ The covalent radius is a measure of the size of an atom.

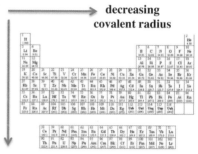

decreasing
covalent radius

increasing
covalent radius

☐ The covalent radius is an example of a periodic property, i.e. with increasing atomic number there is a definite pattern which is repeated across a number of elements (a period), with elements in the same groups generally occurring at the same positions on the "waves".

☐ On crossing a period in the Periodic Table, from left to right, the covalent radius decreases.

☐ On moving from one element to the next, electrons are being added to the same shell and protons are being added to the nucleus. The electrons in the outer shell are therefore attracted more strongly and pulled closer to the nucleus because of its increasing positive charge.

☐ On descending a group in the Periodic Table the covalent radius increases.

☐ On moving from one element to the next, the number of occupied shells is increasing. Although the nuclear charge is increasing, electron shells are progressively distant from the nucleus.

☐ The covalent radius for selected elements is found on page 7 of the Data Booklet.

☐ The size of an ion increases as the number of filled electron shells increases,

e.g. a potassium ion is larger than a sodium ion, a chloride ion is larger than a sodium ion.

☐ For ions with the same number of filled electron shells, the size of an ion decreases with increasing nuclear charge (number of protons),

e.g. a magnesium ion is smaller than a sodium ion, a sodium ion is smaller than a fluoride ion.

☐ The ionic radius for selected ions is found on page 17 of the Data Booklet.

(c) Ionisation energy

☐ The first ionisation energy of an element is the energy required to remove one electron from the outer shell of each atom in one mole of gaseous atoms of the element.

Example: The first ionisation energy of potassium

$$K\,(g) \quad \rightarrow \quad K^+(g) \quad + \quad e^- \qquad \Delta H = +425\ kJ\ mol^{-1}$$

☐ On descending a group in the Periodic Table the first ionisation energy decreases.

increasing ionisation energy →

decreasing ionisation energy

☐ The electron to be removed from the outer shell is increasingly distant from the nucleus as a result of the increasing covalent radius. The attraction of the positive nucleus for that electron diminishes and it therefore becomes easier to remove the electron (less energy is required).

☐ In addition, electrons in the inner shells screen (or shield) those in the outer shell from the full nuclear charge and so lessen the attraction between the nucleus and the electron to be removed. As the number of inner electrons increases, the screening effect increases and consequently it is easier to remove an outer electron (less energy required).

☐ On crossing a period in the Periodic Table, from left to right, there is an increase in the first ionisation energy.

☐ Protons are being added to the nucleus and electrons to the same shell so the outer electrons experience an increasing nuclear charge. This leads to a decrease in covalent radius.

☐ The combination of decreasing covalent radius and increasing nuclear charge means that it is more difficult to remove an outer electron (more energy required).

☐ More than one electron can be removed from an atom and so, in addition to the first ionisation energy, there can also be a second, third, etc. ionisation energy.

☐ The second ionisation energy is the energy required to remove one electron from one mole of one-positive gaseous ions.

Example: The second ionisation energy of magnesium

$$Mg^+ (g) \quad \rightarrow \quad Mg^{2+} (g) \quad + \quad e^- \qquad \Delta H = +1460 \text{ kJ mol}^{-1}$$

☐ The second ionisation energy of a Group 1 metal is much greater than the first ionisation energy since electrons are being removed from a shell closer to the nucleus (greater nuclear pull).

☐ The third ionisation energy is the energy required to remove one electron from one mole of two-positive gaseous ions.

Example: The third ionisation energy of aluminium

$$Al^{2+} (g) \quad \rightarrow \quad Al^{3+} (g) \quad + \quad e^- \qquad \Delta H = +2760 \text{ kJ mol}^{-1}$$

☐ The third ionisation energy of a Group 2 metal is much greater than the second ionisation energy since electrons are being removed from a shell closer to the nucleus (greater nuclear pull).

☐ Ionisation energy is also an example of a periodic property.

☐ The ionisation energies for selected elements are found on page 11 of the Data Booklet.

(d) Electronegativity

☐ Atoms of different elements have different attractions for bonding electrons.

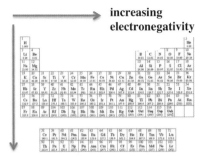

increasing
electronegativity

decreasing
electronegativity

☐ **Electronegativity** is the measure of the attraction that the nucleus of an atom involved in a bond has for the electrons in the bond.

☐ On descending a group in the Periodic Table the electronegativity values decrease.

☐ The bonding electrons are increasingly distant from the nucleus as a result of the increasing covalent radius. The attraction of the positive nucleus for these electrons diminishes.

☐ Electrons in the inner shells will screen (or shield) the bonding electrons from the full nuclear charge and so lessen the attraction between the nucleus and these electrons. As the number of inner electrons increases, the screening effect increases.

☐ On crossing a period in the Periodic Table, from left to right, the electronegativity values increase.

☐ Protons are being added to the nucleus while the bonding electrons are in the same shell. The bonding electrons experience an increasing nuclear charge. The decreasing distance between the bonding electrons and the nucleus increases the attraction of the nucleus for these electrons.

☐ Electronegativity is also an example of a periodic property.

☐ The electronegativity value for selected elements is found on page 11 of the Data Booklet.

3. STRUCTURE AND BONDING

Covalent and ionic bonding (revision)

☐ The noble gases which are in Group 0 of the Periodic Table are made up of atoms that have filled outer shells (energy levels). This is a very stable electron arrangement.

(a) Covalent bonding

☐ When two non-metals join to make a compound, the stable electron arrangement of a noble gas is achieved by atoms sharing electrons.
This sharing of electrons is known as **covalent bonding**.

☐ The shapes of many molecules are based on a tetrahedron.

Examples

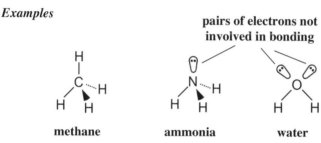

pairs of electrons not
involved in bonding

| methane | ammonia | water |

☐ The protons give a positive charge to the nucleus of the atoms and the electrons give a negative charge to the part of the atom surrounding the nucleus. The merging or overlapping of half-filled clouds to form the covalent bond increases the negative charge in the overlap region. The positive nuclei of both atoms attract the electrons in the overlap region and this holds the atoms together.

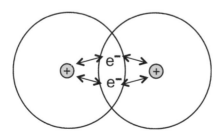

☐ A lot of energy is required to overcome the forces of attraction.
Covalent bonds are therefore strong (100 to 500 kJ mol⁻¹).

☐ Covalent network compounds also exist,

e.g. silicon dioxide and silicon carbide.

☐ Silicon dioxide is found as quartz. Each silicon atom is bonded to four oxygen atoms to give SiO_4 units in the shape of a tetrahedron. These are linked using the oxygen atoms as bridges.

oxygen atom

silicon atom

(b) Ionic bonding

☐ Metals usually react with non-metals to form ionic compounds. The metal atoms lose electrons to achieve the stable electron arrangement of a noble gas thus forming metal ions with a positive charge. The non-metal atoms gain electrons to achieve the stable electron arrangement of a noble gas thus forming non-metal ions with a negative charge. The force of attraction between oppositely charged ions is known as an **ionic bond**.

☐ Atoms of metal elements do not ‘want’ to lose electrons. Energy is required to overcome the force of attraction between the negative outer electron and the positive nucleus (see ‘Ionisation energy’, page 18).

☐ Only a relatively small quantity of energy is released when non-metal atoms gain electrons. This energy alone is not sufficient for the formation of a positive metal ion from a metal atom.

☐ Ionic bonding is a result of the forces of attraction between oppositely charged ions, leading to the formation of an **ionic lattice**. The attractions release large quantities of energy.

Example: In the formation of sodium chloride

$Na^+ (g)$ + $Cl^- (g)$ ➔ $NaCl (s)$

☐ Large amounts of energy are required to overcome the forces of attraction between oppositely charged ions. Ionic bonds are therefore strong (100 to 450 kJ mol^{-1}).

Polar covalent bonds

☐ Pure covalent bonding is mostly found in elements, i.e. when the bonded atoms are identical so that the bonding electrons are shared equally between the atoms,

   e.g. H_2, Cl_2, etc.

☐ In most covalent compounds the bonding is **polar covalent**, i.e. the bonding electrons are not equally shared but are pulled closer to one of the atoms.

☐ Polar covalent bonds arise when there is a difference in the attraction of the nucleus of the atoms for the pair of bonding electrons, i.e. a difference in electronegativity values. This difference is not so great as to lead to ionic bonding. The atom with the higher electronegativity will have a slight negative charge compared to the other atom,

   e.g. chlorine has a higher electronegativity $\delta+$ $\delta-$ | δ *the Greek letter*
   than hydrogen so hydrogen chloride | *'d' for delta means*
   can be represented: $H-Cl$ | *'very small'*

☐ There is therefore a partial permanent positive charge on the hydrogen atoms and a partial permanent negative charge on the chlorine atoms. The molecule is said to have a permanent dipole, i.e. a permanent uneven distribution of charge. In hydrogen chloride, the hydrogen end of the molecule is permanently positive and the chloride end permanently negative.

☐ There are also polar covalent bonds in water. The molecule also has a permanent dipole with the hydrogen end again permanently positive and the oxygen end permanently negative.

$$\delta- \; O \quad \delta+ H \quad H^{\delta+}$$

☐ Carbon and hydrogen atoms have almost the same electronegativity so hydrocarbons have little polarity in the covalent bonds. Carbon and sulphur have the same electronegativity so the bonds in carbon disulphide are non-polar.

☐ While some parts of organic molecules will be (almost) non-polar, other parts may be polar,

   e.g. the carbon chain in hexanol is non-polar but the part of the molecule with the hydroxyl (-OH) group will be polar, making the molecule polar (see 'Alcohols', page 50); an emulsifier molecule is partly polar and partly non-polar (see 'Emulsions in foods', page 65).

A bonding continuum

☐ Pure covalent bonding occurs when the two elements in the bond have the same electronegativity,

e.g. the diatomic elements, carbon disulphide.

☐ If the difference in electronegativity is large, then the movement of bonding electrons from the element of lower electronegativity value towards the element with higher electronegativity value is complete. This results in the formation of ions.

☐ Since metals tend to have low electronegativity values and non-metals tend to have high electronegativity values (see 'Electronegativity', page 20), metals and non-metals, usually, but not always, combine to form ionic bonds,

e.g. typical ionic compounds are sodium chloride, Na^+Cl^-, and magnesium oxide $Mg^{2+}O^{2-}$.

☐ Pure covalent and ionic compounds are opposite ends of a **bonding continuum** with varying degrees of polar covalent bonding lying between these extremes,

e.g. hydrogen fluoride is more polar covalent than hydrogen chloride.

☐ The greater the differences in electronegativity values, the more polar are the bonds that are formed. Even within ionic bonding, there are different degrees of ionic 'character',

e.g. caesium fluoride is more ionic than lithium iodide.

Increasing difference in electronegativity; increasing polarity of a bond

→

| Pure covalent | Polar covalent | Ionic |

Examples

| diatomic elements CS_2 | HCl HF | LiI CsF |

☐ Hydrogen can react with metals. Because of the difference in electronegativity values, ionic compounds containing the hydride ion, H^-, are formed,

e.g. sodium hydride, Na^+H^-, and magnesium hydride, $Mg^{2+}(H^-)_2$.

☐ When there is only a small difference between the electronegativity of the metal and the non-metal in a compound, the bonding may be covalent,

e.g. titanium(IV) chloride is covalent.

Polar molecules

☐ A molecule is described as polar if it has a permanent dipole.

☐ All polar molecules have polar covalent bonds. However, it is necessary to look at the symmetry before predicting whether a molecule is polar.

☐ The molecules are polar when the polar bonds are **not** arranged symmetrically in the molecule. The molecule has a permanent dipole.

Examples

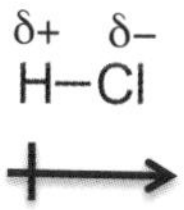

$$\overset{\delta+ \quad \delta-}{H-Cl}$$

hydrogen chloride

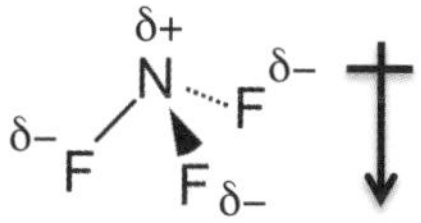

nitrogen fluoride

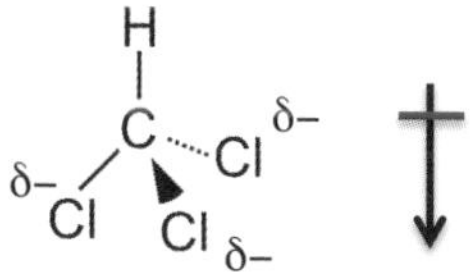

trichloromethane

☐ When there is a symmetrical arrangement of polar bonds and the permanent distribution of charge cancels out, the molecule does **not** have a permanent dipole. The molecule is non-polar.

Example

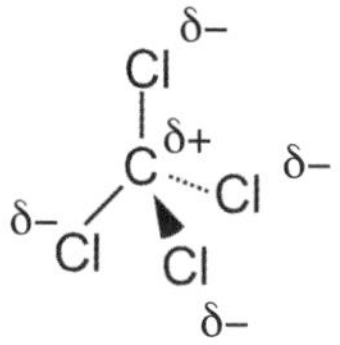

carbon tetrachloride

☐ There is a difference in behaviour between polar and non-polar molecules in an electric field. Polar molecules are attracted by the electric field while non-polar molecules are unaffected.

☐ Where there is little polarity in all the covalent bonds in a molecule, the molecules behave as non-polar,

e.g. hydrocarbons behave as non-polar molecules in an electric field.

Intermolecular forces

☐ All molecular elements and compounds will condense and freeze at sufficiently low temperatures. Monatomic elements (noble gases) will do this as well. For this to occur, some attractive forces must exist between the molecules (or atoms).

☐ The forces of attraction between different molecules are known as **intermolecular forces**. This term is also applied to the forces of attraction between atoms in monatomic elements.

> *Do not confuse **intermolecular** forces (between different molecules) with **intramolecular** forces (within the one molecule).*

☐ All 'intermolecular' forces acting between molecules (or atoms of a noble gas) are known as **van der Waals'** forces.

☐ There are several different types of van der Waals' forces.

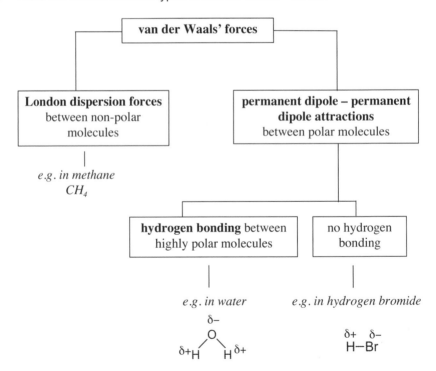

(a) London dispersion forces

☐ London dispersion forces are a type of van der Waals' force. They are forces of attraction between all non-polar molecules (and atoms of the Group 0 elements in the solid or liquid state).

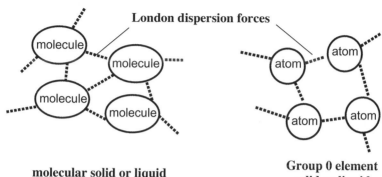

London dispersion forces

molecular solid or liquid

**Group 0 element
solid or liquid**

☐ Since electrons are constantly moving, at any particular moment in time the electron distribution within the molecule (or atom) is unlikely to be evenly spread. Momentarily there may be more negative charge on one side of the molecule (or atom) than on the other. This unequal distribution of charge is called a **dipole**. The London dispersion forces are a result of electrostatic attractions between the **temporary dipoles**.

☐ Since the imbalance of charge is small and non-permanent, London dispersion forces are weak compared to other van der Waals' forces (approximately 4 kJ mol^{-1}).

☐ The strength of the London dispersion forces increases with an increase in the number of electrons within an atom or a molecule. This number of electrons is related to the molecular mass,

e.g the strength of the London dispersion forces increases going down the halogen column in the Periodic Table and with an increasing number of carbon atoms/molecule in the alkanes:

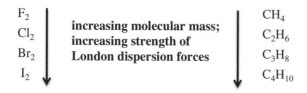

F_2

Cl_2

Br_2

I_2

**increasing molecular mass;
increasing strength of
London dispersion forces**

CH_4

C_2H_6

C_3H_8

C_4H_{10}

(b) Permanent dipole-permanent dipole attractions: not hydrogen bonding

☐ Permanent dipole-permanent dipole attractions are additional forces between polar molecules. There are still London dispersion forces between polar molecules but these are not nearly as significant as the permanent dipole-permanent dipole forces.

☐ Permanent dipole-permanent dipole attractions are another type of van der Waals' force.

☐ A polar molecule will tend to have a permanent dipole due to a difference in electronegativity values between the atoms in the polar covalent bond,

e.g the hydrogen atom in hydrogen bromide has a permanent small positive charge and the bromine atom has a permanent small negative charge, giving rise to a permanent dipole.

$\overset{\delta+}{H}\!\!-\!\!\overset{\delta-}{Br}$

☐ Some molecules with polar bonds do not have a permanent dipole due to the symmetry of the molecule (see 'Polar molecules', page 25). Permanent dipole-permanent dipole attractions do not exist between such molecules.

☐ The permanent dipole-permanent dipole attractions are associated with the polarity of the molecule due to the polar bonds. The small positive charge on an atom in one molecule is attracted to the small negative charge in a different molecule.

☐ Due to the small but permanent charges on atoms in different molecules, permanent dipole-permanent dipole attractions are generally stronger than London dispersion forces.

☐ Since the strength of the London dispersion forces increases with an increase in the number of electrons within an atom or a molecule, for a fair comparison of the strengths of different types of van der Waals' forces, the molecular masses should be approximately the same (see 'Comparing boiling points', pages 32 and 33).

(c) Permanent dipole-permanent dipole attractions: hydrogen bonding

☐ For a non-metal, hydrogen has a very low electronegativity value. Bonds consisting of a hydrogen atom bonded to an atom of a highly electronegative element will be highly polar.

☐ The relatively strong electrostatic forces of attraction between molecules that contain these highly polar bonds, i.e. highly polar molecules, are known as **hydrogen bonds**.

☐ Since fluorine, nitrogen and oxygen are highly electronegative elements, the covalent bonds between these elements and hydrogen give rise to strong permanent dipoles.

Examples

hydrogen fluoride   **ammonia**   **water**

☐ Hydrogen bonding occurs in water.

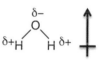

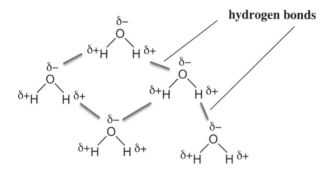

☐ A hydrogen bond is stronger than all other permanent dipole-permanent dipole attractions (approximately 30 kJ mol^{-1}) but weaker than a covalent bond.

☐ Hydrogen bonds are another type of van der Waals' force.

4. PROPERTIES OF COMPOUNDS

☐ The type of bonding in a compound is related to the difference in electronegativity between atoms of the constituent elements. This difference depends on the relative positions of the elements in the Periodic Table.

☐ The properties of a compound are related to the type of bonding and structure.

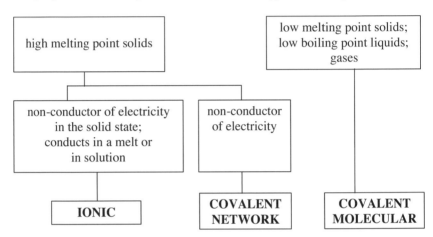

☐ It is the properties of a compound that should be used to deduce the type of bonding and structure rather the types of elements present in the formula,

e.g. TiCl$_4$ has a melting point of -24°C; although it is made from a metal and a non-metal element, the relatively low melting point indicates that the bonding is covalent.

(a) Electrical conductivity

☐ Ionic compounds do not conduct electricity in the solid state because the ions are not free to move. Ionic compounds do conduct when in the liquid state or when dissolved in water. The decomposition of a melt or a solution by the movement of ions is called **electrolysis**.

☐ Covalent molecular and covalent network compounds do not conduct electricity.

(b) Melting and boiling points

(i) Compounds with relatively high melting and boiling points

☐ Ionic compounds have high melting and boiling points. A lot of energy is required to separate the oppositely charged ions in the lattice.

☐ Covalent network compounds have high melting points because covalent bonds are broken on melting and a lot of energy is required for this.

(ii) Compounds with relatively low melting and boiling points

☐ Melting points and boiling points increase as the strength of the intermolecular forces that occur between molecules increases.

☐ The strength of the intermolecular forces increases as the number of electrons present in the molecule increases, i.e. the strength of the intermolecular forces increases with increasing molecular mass,

   *e.g. the melting and boiling points of the halogens (non-polar molecules) increase going down the group due to increasing molecular mass; at room temperature, **fluorine** is a **gas**, **bromine** is a **liquid** and **iodine** is a **solid**.*

☐ Non-polar substances with a high molecular mass may be a solid at room temperature due to the strength of the intermolecular forces.

   e.g. camphor ($C_{10}H_{16}O$) with a molecular mass of 152 is a solid at room temperature.

☐ The strength of the intermolecular forces (and hence boiling point) is related to the type of van der Waals' force.

London dispersion forces	Permanent dipole – permanent dipole attractions	
	not hydrogen bonding	hydrogen bonding
non-polar atoms and molecules	**Increasing polarity of molecules** →	highly polar molecule
weaker intermolecular forces	**Increasing strength** →	strong intermolecular forces
lower boiling point	**Increasing boiling point** →	higher boiling point

Comparing boiling points: butane and propanone

☐ Butane with a relative molecular mass of 58 does not have polar bonds. Molecules of butane are non-polar.

$$H-\overset{\overset{H}{|}}{\underset{\underset{H}{|}}{C}}-\overset{\overset{H}{|}}{\underset{\underset{H}{|}}{C}}-\overset{\overset{H}{|}}{\underset{\underset{H}{|}}{C}}-\overset{\overset{H}{|}}{\underset{\underset{H}{|}}{C}}-H$$

☐ The intermolecular forces in liquid butane are the weak London dispersion forces.

London dispersion forces

☐ Propanone, also with a relative molecular mass of 58, has a polar bond. Molecules of propanone are polar due to the permanent dipole.

$$CH_3-\overset{\overset{\delta-}{O}}{\underset{\underset{\delta+}{\|}}{C}}-CH_3$$

☐ The permanent dipole-permanent dipole attractions associated with the $\overset{\delta+}{C}=\overset{\delta-}{O}$ bond are stronger than the London dispersion forces.

permanent dipole – permanent dipole attractions

☐ The stronger intermolecular forces are responsible for the relatively high boiling point of propanone (56 °C) compared with butane (0 °C).

☐ The boiling points can be used to compare the types of intermolecular forces in butane and propanone since butane and propanone both have a molecular mass of 58. The impact of the London dispersion forces will be the same.

Comparing boiling points: ethanol and propane

☐ The intermolecular forces in ethanol (molecular mass 46) are relatively strong hydrogen bonds.

hydrogen bonding

☐ The intermolecular forces in liquid propane (molecular mass 44) are the weak London dispersion forces.

London dispersion forces

☐ As a result, the boiling point of ethanol (72°C) can be predicted to be higher than propane (-42°C).

Comparing the boiling points of hydrogen compounds

☐ The boiling points of the Group 4 hydrides decrease from stannane (SnH_4) to methane (CH_4). This decrease is an expected one in view of the fact that the molecules are non-polar and the London dispersion forces are becoming weaker with a decrease in the number of electrons in the molecules (molecular mass).

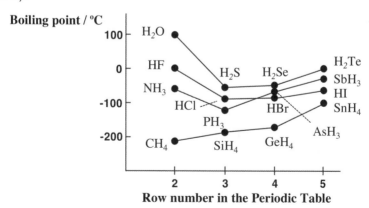

☐ There is a similar and expected decrease in boiling point from hydrogen telluride (H_2Te) though hydrogen selenide (H_2Se) to hydrogen sulphide (H_2S) but water has a much higher boiling point than might have been anticipated.

☐ Water is made up of highly polar molecules. **Hydrogen bonding** accounts for the unexpected high boiling point. Considerable energy is required to overcome the relatively strong intermolecular forces.

☐ A similar pattern emerges with the hydrides of the Group 5 and Group 7 elements where the boiling points for ammonia (NH_3) and hydrogen fluoride (HF) are much higher than extrapolation of the plots would suggest.

☐ Liquid ammonia and liquid hydrogen fluoride are made up of highly polar molecules. **Hydrogen bonding** accounts for their unexpected high boiling points.

☐ In hydrogen fluoride the relatively strong forces of attraction between the hydrogen atoms and the fluorine atoms of neighbouring molecules in the liquid and solid states results in long hydrogen bonded chains.

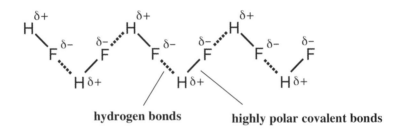

hydrogen bonds   **highly polar covalent bonds**

(c) Density of water

☐ The density of water increases as the temperature falls to 4 °C but from 4 °C to 0 °C the density decreases with the formation of ice. The water molecules begin to move further apart to form an open and rigid structure held together by hydrogen bonds.

☐ The fact that ice is less dense than water means that ponds and rivers will freeze from the surface downwards and the layer of ice insulates the water below, thus preventing complete solidification and allowing plant-life and fish-life to continue.

(d) Viscosity

☐ The **viscosity** of a liquid is a measure of its resistance to flow. In everyday terms, it can be thought of as the "thickness",

e.g. water is "thin" but honey is "thick".

☐ Viscosity is another property of substances that is related to the type of intermolecular force that exists between molecules. Liquids with strong intermolecular forces between the molecules are likely to have a high viscosity (to be viscous).

☐ Molecules with −OH groups have hydrogen bonding between the molecules.

$$\delta + \quad \delta -$$
$$\overset{\delta -}{-O} \cdots \overset{}{H}-O-$$
$$\overset{}{\underset{H^{\delta +}}{}}$$

Examples

glycerol (propan-1,2,3-triol) has 3 –OH groups per molecule

$$CH_2-OH$$
$$|$$
$$CH-OH$$
$$|$$
$$CH_2-OH$$

ethylene glycol (ethane-1,2-diol) has 2 –OH groups per molecule

$$CH_2-OH$$
$$|$$
$$CH_2-OH$$

methanol has 1 –OH group per molecule

$$CH_3-OH$$

☐ The strength of the hydrogen bonds increases with an increase in the number of the -OH groups/molecule. As a result, glycerol is the most viscous of the three liquids and methanol the least viscous.

☐ Propanone has permanent dipole-permanent dipole attractions between molecules. These intermolecular forces are not as strong as hydrogen bonds. With weaker intermolecular forces, propanone is less viscous than methanol, ethanol and propanol.

$$CH_3-\overset{\overset{O}{\parallel}}{C}-CH_3$$

(e) Solubility

(i) Ionic (and polar) compounds

☐ In a solution, the solute is the substance that is dissolved and the solvent is what the solute has dissolved in,

e.g. in an aqueous salt solution, salt is the solute and water is the solvent.

☐ Ionic compounds are soluble in water.
This is a result of the polar nature of the water molecules.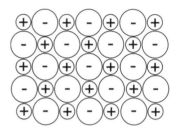

☐ Energy is required to separate the oppositely charged ions in an ionic lattice.

☐ The slight negative ends of the polar water molecules are attracted to the positive ions in the lattice while the slight positive ends of the water molecules are attracted to the negative ions. The electrostatic attractions between the ions and the water molecules result in a release of energy and the formation of **hydrated** ions. This energy is sufficient to overcome the electrostatic attractions between the oppositely charged ions in the lattice.

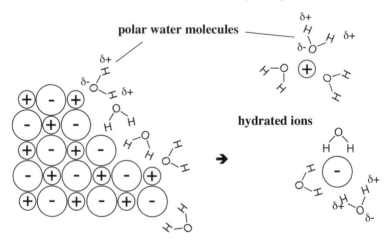

polar water molecules

hydrated ions

☐ Ionic compounds are likely to be soluble in other polar solvents for similar reasons,

e.g. salt is slightly soluble in ethanol.

☐ Polar molecular compounds also tend to be soluble in water,

e.g. ethanol and propanone are soluble in water.

☐ Energy is required to overcome the forces of attraction associated with the hydrogen bonds between molecules in water and the intermolecular attractions between molecules in ethanol and propanone.

$$CH_3-\overset{\overset{\displaystyle O}{\|}}{\underset{\delta+}{C}}-CH_3$$

$$CH_3-CH_2-O^{\delta-}\diagdown H^{\delta+}$$

energy released in formation of new intermolecular bonds

☐ Sufficient energy is released by the electrostatic attractions between the dissolving polar molecules and polar water molecules to overcome the forces of attraction in the water and any in the dissolving molecules.

☐ Ionic and polar molecular compounds are less likely to be soluble in non-polar solvents,

e.g. sodium chloride and ethanol are less likely to be soluble in hexane.

☐ Interactions between the ions (or polar molecules) and the non-polar solvent molecules would be so weak that insufficient energy would be released to overcome the ionic bonds (or forces of attraction between polar molecules).

☐ Compounds made up of molecules with relatively low polarity are insoluble in water,

e.g. ester are insoluble in water (see 'Uses of esters', page 58).

☐ When ester molecules bond with water molecules the energy released is insufficient to overcome the strong hydrogen bonds in water.

(ii) Non-polar substances

☐ Generally, non-polar substances dissolve in non-polar solvents but are insoluble in polar solvents,

e.g. iodine is soluble in hexane but does not readily dissolve in water.

☐ Little energy is required to overcome both the weak London dispersion forces between the hexane molecules in the solvent and also those in the iodine solid. Sufficient energy is released to do this when iodine molecules set up London dispersion forces with hexane molecules.

☐ Insufficient energy would be released in setting up London dispersion forces between iodine molecules and water molecules in order to overcome the stronger hydrogen bonds between the water molecules.

Solubility summary

☐ The table below gives a guide to solubility of substances in different types of solvent.

Substance	Water (and other polar solvents)	Non-polar solvents
Ionic	more likely to be soluble	less likely to be soluble
Polar molecular	more likely to be soluble	less likely to be soluble
Non-polar molecular	less likely to be soluble	more likely to be soluble

Examples

$$HO-CH_2-\overset{\overset{\displaystyle OH}{|}}{CH}-\overset{\overset{\displaystyle OH}{|}}{CH}-C\overset{\displaystyle\nearrow O}{\underset{\displaystyle\searrow OH}{}}$$

erythrose (polar molecule)

More likely to be soluble in an alcohol and water (both polar) than hexane (non-polar).

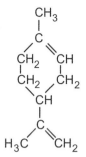

More likely to be soluble in hexane (non-polar) than an alcohol or water (both polar).

limonene (non-polar molecule)

☐ Polar molecules (solvent and solute) can be identified by $-OH$ (hydroxyl), $-NH_2$ (amino), $-C\!\!\overset{O}{\underset{OH}{}}$ (carboxyl) or $-\overset{O}{\underset{}{C}}-$ (carbonyl) groups.

Non-polar molecules with polar bonds

☐ Some solvents have molecules with polar bonds but cannot be classified as a polar solvent due to the symetrical arrangement of bonds in the molecule (see 'Polar molecules', page 25),

e.g. tetrachloromethane.

☐ Ionic compounds and polar molecular compounds are less likely to be soluble in these non-polar solvents,

e.g. sodium chloride is insoluble in tetrachloromethane.

☐ Non-polar substances are more likely to be soluble in such solvents,

e.g. iodine is soluble in tetrachloromethane.

(e) Hardness

☐ Covalent compounds with network structures tend to be very hard due to the network of strong covalent bonds,

e.g. silicon dioxide and silicon carbide.

☐ Silicon carbide is found as carborundum. It is used as an abrasive and the cutting and grinding of the surfaces of tools.

Ionisation in water

☐ Hydrogen chloride is a covalent gas at room temperature, HCl (g). The bonds in hydrogen chloride are polar covalent.

$$\overset{\delta+ \quad \delta-}{H-Cl}$$

☐ When hydrogen chloride reacts with water, energy is released when the attractions are set up between the hydrogen chloride molecules and the polar water molecules. This energy is more than sufficient to break the covalent bonds in all the hydrogen chloride molecules.

$$\overset{\delta-}{O}\cdots\overset{\delta+\quad\delta-}{H-Cl}\cdots\overset{\delta+}{H}\quad H$$

$$H^+(aq) \quad + \quad Cl^-(aq)$$

☐ Hydrogen chloride therefore completely ionises in water to form an acidic solution. This explains why an aqueous solution of hydrogen chloride, HCl (aq), is a good conductor of electricity.

☐ Other polar covalent substances completely ionise in water to form acidic solutions,

e.g. the other hydrogen halides, HF (g), HBr (g), HI (g) and pure concentrated sulphuric acid, H_2SO_4 (l).

Unit 2   Nature's Chemistry

1. HYDROCARBONS (revision)

Naming and the structure of the alkanes

☐ The **alkanes** are a subset of the set of hydrocarbons. Each member of the series has a name which ends in -**ane** and a prefix that indicates the number of carbon atoms in the molecule.

Prefix	Number of C atoms		Prefix	Number of C atoms
meth-	1		pent-	5
eth-	2		hex-	6
prop-	3		hept-	7
but-	4		oct-	8

☐ The **full structural formula** can be used to show the arrangement of atoms.

☐ A **shortened structural formula** can be used to show the grouping of hydrogen atoms round each carbon.

Example

Number of carbon atoms in the molecule	4
Name of alkane	butane
Formula	C_4H_{10}
Full structural formula	$\begin{array}{c} \text{H} \quad \text{H} \quad \text{H} \quad \text{H} \\ \mid \quad \mid \quad \mid \quad \mid \\ \text{H}-\text{C}-\text{C}-\text{C}-\text{C}-\text{H} \\ \mid \quad \mid \quad \mid \quad \mid \\ \text{H} \quad \text{H} \quad \text{H} \quad \text{H} \end{array}$
Shortened structural formula	$CH_3-CH_2-CH_2-CH_3$ or $CH_3CH_2CH_2CH_3$

☐ All alkanes are **saturated** hydrocarbons, i.e. all the carbon to carbon bonds are single covalent bonds.

☐ There are three different structures for alkanes with molecular formula C_5H_{12}. Shortened structural formulae are shown below.

A $CH_3-CH_2-CH_2-CH_2-CH_3$

B $CH_3-CH-CH_2-CH_3$
$\quad\quad\;\; |$
$\quad\quad\; CH_3$

C $CH_3-\underset{\underset{\textstyle CH_3}{|}}{\overset{\overset{\textstyle CH_3}{|}}{C}}-CH_3$

Structure **A** is called a **straight chain** hydrocarbon, i.e. all the carbon atoms are joined to two or one (at end) neighbouring carbon atoms. Structures **B** and **C** are called **branched-chain** hydrocarbons, i.e. one (or more) of the carbon atoms is joined to three or four neighbouring carbon atoms.

☐ Branches are named after the corresponding alkanes with the ‑ane ending changed to **–yl**.

Examples

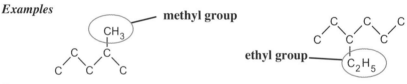

methyl group

ethyl group

To name a branched chain alkane:

1. Select the longest continuous chain of carbon atoms and name it after the appropriate alkane.
2. Number the carbon atoms from the end of the chain nearer the branch.
3. Name the branch(es) and indicate the position(s) of the branch(es) on the chain with the number(s) of the carbon atoms(s).
4. Use 'di' and 'tri' , etc. when the same branch is present more than once.

Examples

$CH_3-CH_2-CH_2-\underset{\underset{\textstyle CH_3}{|}}{CH}-CH_3$
⑤　④　③　②　①

2-methylpentane

① CH_3
　　|　　③　④　⑤
② $CH_2-\underset{\underset{\textstyle CH_3}{|}}{CH}-CH_2-CH_3$

3-methylpentane

$CH_3-\underset{\underset{\textstyle CH_3}{|}}{\overset{\overset{\textstyle CH_3}{|}}{CH}}-\overset{\overset{\textstyle CH_3}{|}}{CH}-CH_3$
④　　③　　②　　①

2,3-dimethylbutane

☐ Saturated hydrocarbons with a ring of carbon atoms are called **cycloalkanes**.

Example

Number of carbon atoms in the molecule	6
Name of cycloalkane	cyclohexane
Formula	C_6H_{12}
Full structural formula	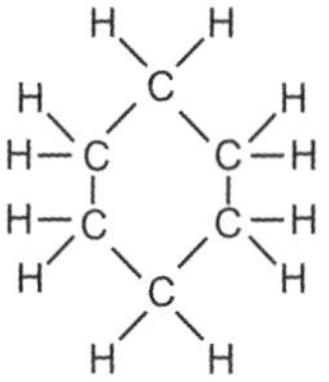
Shortened structural formula	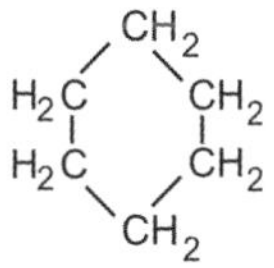

☐ Like the alkanes, the cycloalkanes are **saturated** hydrocarbons.

☐ With branched-chain cycloalkanes, the positions of two or more branches are given by numbers.

Examples

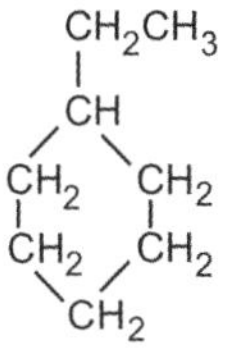

ethylcyclohexane

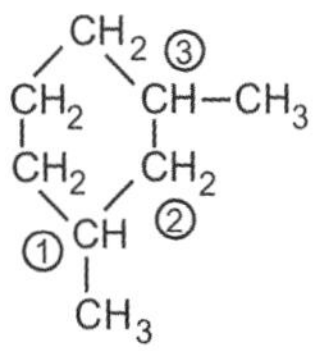

1,3-dimethylcyclohexane

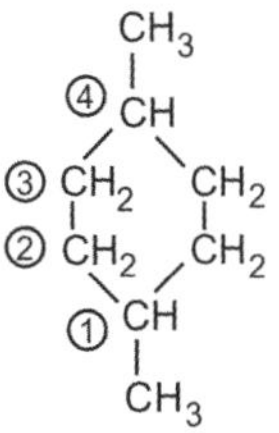

1,4-dimethylcyclohexane

Naming and the structure of the alkenes

☐ The alkenes are also a subset of the set of hydrocarbons. Each member of the series has a name which ends in **-ene** and a prefix that indicates the number of carbon atoms in the molecule.

Example

Number of carbon atoms in the molecule	3
Name of alkene	propene
Formula	C_3H_6
Full structural formula	
Shortened structural formula	$CH_2{=}CH - CH_3$ or $CH_2 CH CH_3$

☐ All alkenes are **unsaturated** hydrocarbons, i.e. there is at least one carbon to carbon double bond in an alkene.

☐ The carbon to carbon double bond is an example of a group of atoms with characteristic properties.

☐ Branched-chain alkenes are named in a similar way to alkanes.

1 Select the longest continuous chain of carbon atoms containing the double bond and name it after the appropriate alkene.

2. Number the carbon atoms from the end of the chain nearer the double bond and indicate the position of the double bond with the lowest number of carbon atom at the double bond.

3. Name any branch(es) and indicate the position(s) of the branch(es) on the chain with the number(s) of the carbon atom(s).

Examples

but-1-ene   **but-2-ene**

3-methylbut-1-ene

☐ Unsaturated hydrocarbons can also form a ring of carbon atoms.

$$\begin{array}{c} CH_2 \\ \diagup \quad \diagdown \\ CH \qquad CH_2 \\ \| \qquad \qquad | \\ CH \qquad CH_2 \\ \diagdown \quad \diagup \\ CH_2 \end{array}$$

cyclohexene

Reactions of alkenes

☐ When bromine (in solution) is added to an alkene, the bromine is immediately decolourised. There is no immediate reaction when bromine is added to an alkane. In the reaction of bromine with the alkene, the carbon to carbon double bond breaks and the bromine atoms add on the carbon atoms at either side of this bond.

Example 1:   The reaction of ethene with bromine

$$\begin{array}{cc} H \diagdown \qquad \diagup H \\ \qquad C = C \\ H \diagup \qquad \diagdown H \end{array} \quad + \ \ Br_2 \ \ \longrightarrow \quad \begin{array}{c} H \quad H \\ | \quad | \\ H - C - C - H \\ | \quad | \\ Br \quad Br \end{array}$$

Example 2:   The reaction of propene with bromine

$$\begin{array}{c} H \quad H \quad H \\ H \diagdown \quad | \quad | \\ \quad C = C - C - H \\ H \diagup \qquad | \\ \qquad H \end{array} \quad + \ \ Br_2 \ \ \longrightarrow \quad \begin{array}{c} H \quad H \quad H \\ | \quad | \quad | \\ H - C - C - C - H \\ | \quad | \quad | \\ Br \quad Br \quad H \end{array}$$

☐ This type of reaction is called an **addition reaction** because of the way that bromine adds on to the alkene.

☐ The reaction with bromine is the way to distinguish any unsaturated hydrocarbon from a saturated hydrocarbon. The bromine is immediately decolourised by the unsaturated hydrocarbon.

☐ Alkenes can also react with hydrogen in an addition reaction. The corresponding alkane is formed.

Example: The reaction of ethene with hydrogen

$$\begin{array}{cc} H \diagdown \qquad \diagup H \\ \qquad C = C \\ H \diagup \qquad \diagdown H \end{array} \quad + \ \ H_2 \ \ \longrightarrow \quad \begin{array}{c} H \quad H \\ | \quad | \\ H - C - C - H \\ | \quad | \\ H \quad H \end{array}$$

ethene   ethane

Homologous series

☐ A homologous series is a family of compounds that can be represented by a general formula.

☐ The general formula for the **alkanes** is C_nH_{2n+2}. Each of the alkanes has two hydrogen atoms for every carbon atom plus one additional hydrogen at each end.

☐ The general formula for the **alkenes** is C_nH_{2n}. Each of the alkenes has two hydrogen atoms less than the corresponding alkane due to the double covalent bond.

☐ The general formula for the **cycloalkanes** is also C_nH_{2n}. Each of the cycloalkanes has two hydrogen atoms less than the corresponding alkane due to the bond that closes the ring.

☐ Successive members in a series differ in formula by a $-CH_2$ group and as a result the relative formula masses differ by 14.

☐ Physical properties of compounds in a homologous series show a gradual change from one member to the next,

   e.g. boiling point.

☐ Chemical properties of compounds in a homologous series are very similar,

   e.g. all alkenes react with bromine.

☐ However, chemical properties can be used to distinguish between hydrocarbons in different series,

   e.g. although alkenes and cycloalkanes have the same general formula, alkenes react with bromine but cycloalkanes do not (see 'Reactions of alkenes', page 45).

Isomers

☐ **Isomers** are compounds with the same molecular formula but different structures.

☐ The following flow diagram can be used to decide whether or not two compounds are isomers.

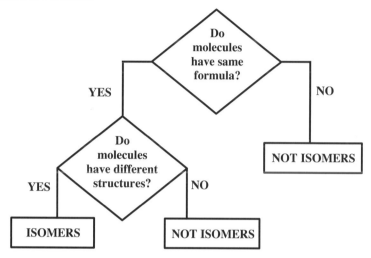

Examples

1. $CH_3-CH_2-CH_3$ CH_3-CH_3 **different formulae**
    NOT isomers

    propane   **ethane**

2. $\overset{\displaystyle CH_3}{\underset{}{CH_3-CH-CH_2-CH_3}}$ $\underset{\displaystyle CH_3}{CH_3-CH_2-CH-CH_3}$ **same formula**
    same structure
    NOT isomers

    methylbutane   **methylbutane**

3. $\overset{\displaystyle CH_3}{\underset{\displaystyle CH_3}{CH_3-C-CH_3}}$ $\underset{\displaystyle CH_3}{CH_3-CH-CH_2-CH_3}$ **same formula**
    different structures
    isomers

    dimethylpropane   **methylbutane**

    > *It is not necessary to number the methyl group(s) in methylbutane and dimethylpropane.*

4. $CH_2=CH-CH_2-CH_3$ $CH_3-CH=CH-CH_3$ same formula
different structures
but-1-ene   **but-2-ene**   isomers

5. $CH_2=CH-CH_2-CH_3$ $CH_3-CH_2-CH=CH_2$ same formula
same structure
but-1-ene   **but-1-ene**   NOT isomers

6. $CH_3-CH=CH_2$ same formula
$\overset{CH_2}{\underset{CH_2-CH_2}{\diagdown}}$ different structures
propene   isomers
cyclopropane

> *Isomers need not be in the same homolgous series.*

☐ Many carbon compounds, other than hydrocarbons, have isomers.

Examples

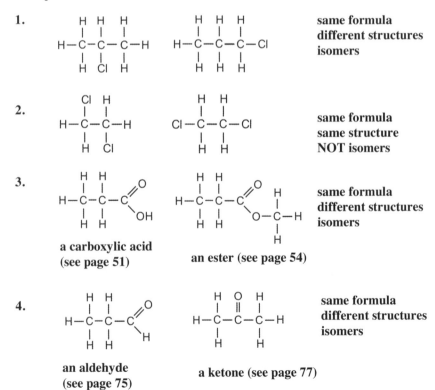

1. same formula
different structures
isomers

2. same formula
same structure
NOT isomers

3. a carboxylic acid
(see page 51)   an ester (see page 54)   same formula
different structures
isomers

4. an aldehyde
(see page 75)   a ketone (see page 77)   same formula
different structures
isomers

2. ALCOHOLS, CARBOXYLIC ACIDS AND ESTERS

(a) The alcohols

Naming and structure

☐ The **hydroxyl group** (-OH) is the group that gives the characteristic properties to the alcohols. The atoms in a hydroxyl group are joined by a covalent bond and the group is part of a covalent molecule.

> *Do not confuse a hydroxyl group with a hydroxide ion, OH⁻ (aq), found in alkalis.*

☐ A group that that gives characteristic properties to families of carbon compounds is called a **functional group**.

☐ Straight chain alcohols take their name from the corresponding alkane. Each member of the series has a name that ends in **-anol** and a prefix that indicates the number of carbon atoms in the molecule,

e.g. *ethanol has the hydroxyl group attached to a chain of two carbon atoms:*

$$-\overset{|}{\underset{|}{C}}-\overset{|}{\underset{|}{C}}-OH$$

☐ The different ways of representing ethanol are shown below.

Full structural formula	Shortened structural formula	Formula
$H-\overset{\overset{H}{\mid}}{\underset{\underset{H}{\mid}}{C}}-\overset{\overset{H}{\mid}}{\underset{\underset{H}{\mid}}{C}}-OH$	CH_3-CH_2-OH or $CH_3\,CH_2-OH$ or CH_3CH_2OH	C_2H_5OH

☐ From propanol onwards, the hydroxyl group can be in different positions in the carbon chain.

☐ To name an alcohol:

  1 Select the longest continuous chain of carbon atoms containing the hydroxyl group and name it after the appropriate alkane.

  2 Number the carbon atoms from the end of the chain nearer the hydroxyl group and indicate the position of the hydroxyl group.

  3 Name any branch(es) and indicate the position(s) of the branch(es) on the chain.

Examples

③ ② ①
$CH_3-CH_2-CH_2-OH$

propan-1-ol

① ② ③
$CH_3-CH-CH_3$
     |
    OH

propan-2-ol

> *Propan-1-ol and propan-2-ol are isomers.*

④ ③ ② ①
$CH_3-CH-CH_2-CH_2-OH$
     |
    CH_3

3-methylbutan-1-ol

Polarity of molecules

☐ Alcohols are polar molecules due to the presence of the hydroxyl group (see 'Polar covalent bonds', page 23).

       | δ- δ+
    $-C-O-H$
       |

☐ The polarity of the molecule gives rise to hydrogen bonding between molecules (see 'Intermolecular forces', page 29). The intermolecular forces associated with hydrogen bonding are relatively strong and have an impact on the properties of alcohols,

e.g. the relatively high boiling point (for molecular mass), solubility in water (see 'Properties of compounds', pages 33 and 37).

Industrial manufacture

☐ Ethanol can be prepared in industry by the reaction of ethene with water. Since the double bond breaks as the atoms in water are added on to the carbon atom at either side, this is another example of an **addition reaction**.

     ethene   **water**   **ethanol**

☐ This type of reaction is also known as **hydration**.

> *Do not confuse a hydration reaction with a **hydrolysis** reaction. In a hydrolysis reaction, the addition of the atoms of water results in the molecule splitting into two parts (see 'Breaking of esters', page 57, 'Fats and oils', page 60 and 'Breaking of proteins', page 68).*

Alcohols with more than one hydroxyl group in a molecule

☐ Alcohols with two hydroxyl groups in a molecule are called **diols**; alcohols with three hydroxyl groups in a molecule are called **triols**.

Examples

$$CH_2-CH_2$$
$$\ \ |\qquad\ |$$
$$OH\quad OH$$

ethane-1,2-diol
(ethylene glycol)

$$CH_2-CH-CH_2$$
$$\ \ |\qquad\ |\qquad\ |$$
$$OH\quad OH\quad OH$$

propane-1,2,3-triol
(glycerol)

☐ The increased polarity of diols and triols results in stronger hydrogen bonding and higher boiling points (for molecules of similar mass).

	Molecular mass	Boiling point / °C
ethane-1,2-diol	62	197
propan-1-ol	60	97
propane-1,2,3-triol	92	290
pentan-1-ol	88	137

(b) Carboxylic acids

Naming and structure

☐ The group that gives the characteristic properties to the carboxylic acids is the **carboxyl** group:

$$-C\!\!\begin{array}{c}{\scriptstyle /\!\!/O}\\{\scriptstyle \backslash OH}\end{array}$$

☐ Each member of the carboxylic acid homologous series has a name that ends in **-anoic acid** and a prefix that indicates the number of carbon atoms in the molecule,

e.g. ethanoic acid has two carbon atoms including the carbon in the carboxylic acid group:

$$-C-C\!\!\begin{array}{c}{\scriptstyle /\!\!/O}\\{\scriptstyle \backslash OH}\end{array}$$

☐ The characteristic acid group must always be at the end of a carbon chain.

☐ The different ways of representing ethanoic acid are shown below.

Full structural formula	Shortened structural formula	Formula
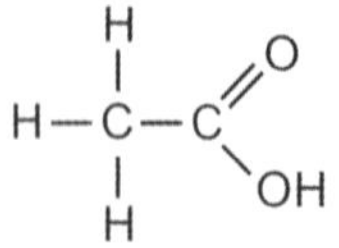	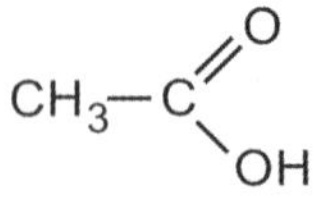 or $CH_3{-}COOH$ or CH_3COOH	CH_3COOH

☐ With branched chain carboxylic acids, any branch(es) and the position(s) of the branch(es) on the chain are named in the same way as with alcohols.

Examples

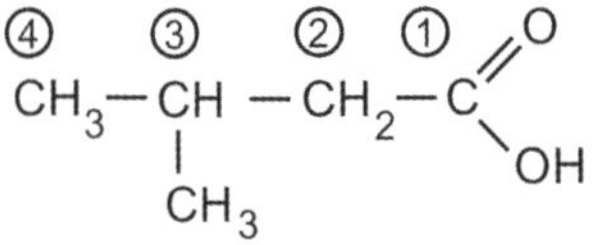

3-methylbutanoic acid

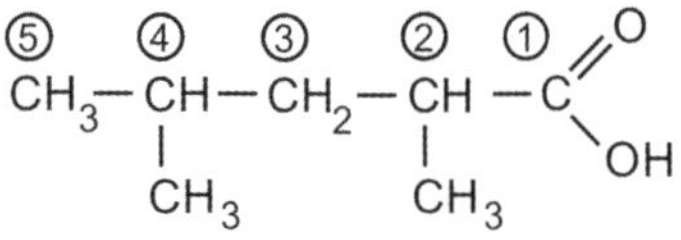

2,4-dimethylpentanoic acid

Reactions of carboxylic acids

☐ When carboxylic acids are in aqueous solution, there is an equilibrium between molecules of the acid and positive hydrogen ions and negative carboxylate ions. The carboxylate ions take their name from the acid with the 'oic' ending changed to '**oate**'.

Example: ethanoic acid

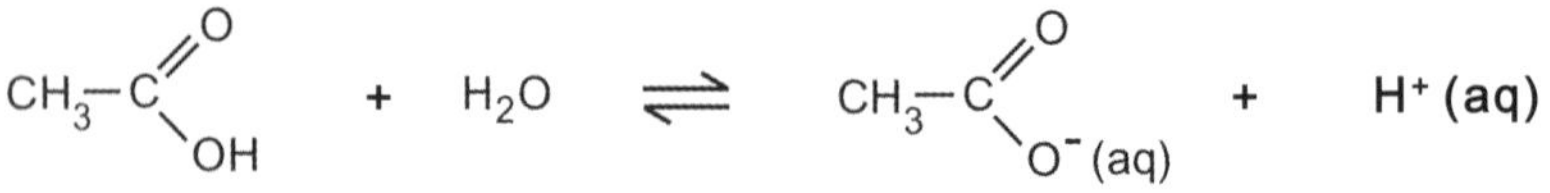

molecules of acid   **ethanoate ions**   **hydrogen ions**

☐ The ' ⇌ ' sign shows that the dissociation (breaking up) of ethanoic acid molecules in aqueous solution is a **reversible** reaction that can eventually reach **equilibrium** (see 'Equilibrium' , page 115).

(i) Reaction with bases

☐ As with other acids, the hydrogen ion, H^+ (aq), reacts with a base to form a salt and water. This type of reaction is an example of **neutralisation**.
Salts of carboxylic acids contain the carboxylate ion.

Example: *The reaction of ethanoic acid with a metal oxide*

$$2CH_3COOH \quad + \quad CaO \quad \rightarrow \quad (CH_3COO^-)_2Ca^{2+} \quad + \quad H_2O$$

ethanoic acid   calcium oxide   calcium ethanoate   water

Example: *The reaction of methanoic acid with an alkali*

$$HCOOH \quad + \quad NaOH \quad \rightarrow \quad HCOO^-Na^+ \quad + \quad H_2O$$

methanoic   sodium   sodium   water
acid   hydroxide   methanoate

Example: *The reaction of propanoic acid with a metal carbonate*

$$2CH_3CH_2COOH \quad + \quad CuCO_3 \quad \rightarrow \quad (CH_3CH_2COO^-)_2Cu^{2+} \quad + \quad H_2O \quad + \quad CO_2$$

propanoic   copper(II)   copper(II)   water   carbon
acid   carbonate   propanoate   dioxide

(ii) Reaction with metals

☐ Carboxylic acids react with metals above hydrogen in the electrochemical series. The products are salts containing the carboxylate ion and hydrogen gas.

Example: *The reaction of ethanoic acid with magnesium*

$$2CH_3COOH \quad + \quad Mg \quad \rightarrow \quad (CH_3COO^-)_2Mg^{2+} \quad + \quad H_2$$

ethanoic acid   magnesium   magnesium   hydrogen
ethanoate

This is an example of a **redox reaction**.

oxidation $Mg(s) \quad \rightarrow \quad Mg^{2+}(aq) \quad + \quad 2e^-$

reduction $2H^+(aq) \quad + \quad 2e^- \quad \rightarrow \quad H_2(g)$

(c) Esters

Naming and structure

☐ **Esters** are covalent compounds with the molecules containing carbon, hydrogen and oxygen atoms.

☐ They are the products of reactions between **alcohols** and **carboxylic acids**. An ester takes its name from the alcohol and carboxylic acid from which it can be made. The name contains the ending **-yl** (from the alcohol) and **-oate** (from the carboxylic acid). The alcohol part of the name always comes first.

> *Example*   alcohol: methanol   acid: ethanoic
>
> ester: **methyl**   ester: **ethanoate**
>
> name: **methyl ethanoate**

☐ Since esters are prepared from alcohols and carboxylic acids, all esters contain the characteristic group:

Note that the alcohol part of the structure has been turned round.

☐ When written the other way round, the group looks like:

Note that the acid part of the structure has been turned round.

☐ Esters can be named from their structure.

The side of the structure with the $\diagdown$C=O must come from the acid.

Example 1

from alcohol   **from acid**

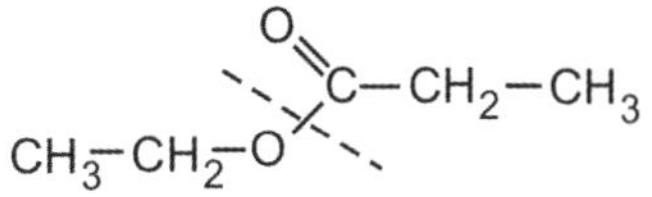

$$CH_3{-}CH_2{-}O$$

alcohol:	ethanol	acid:	propanoic
ester:	**ethyl**	ester:	**propanoate**
name:	**ethyl propanoate**		

Example 2

from acid   **from alcohol**

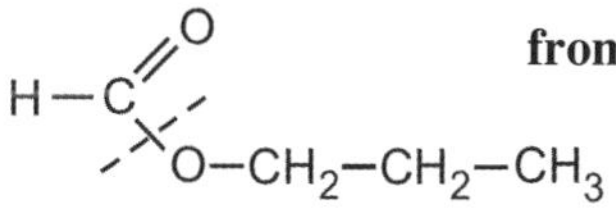

alcohol:	propanol	acid:	methanoic
ester:	**propyl**	ester:	**methanoate**
name:	**propyl methanoate**		

Making esters

☐ Esters are formed by the reactions of alcohols with carboxylic acids.

Example: **The reaction between ethanoic acid and methanol**

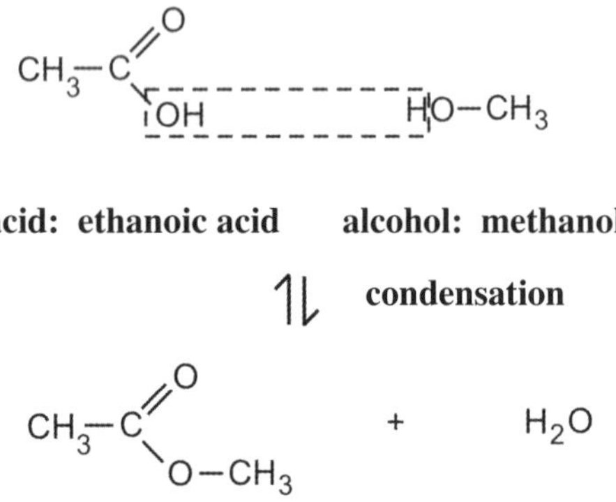

$$CH_3-C \overset{\displaystyle O}{\underset{\overline{OH}}{\diagup}} \quad - - - - - - - - - - \quad \overline{H}O-CH_3$$

acid: ethanoic acid   alcohol: methanol

⇅ **condensation**

$$CH_3-C \overset{\displaystyle O}{\diagdown} \quad + \quad H_2O$$
$$O-CH_3$$

ester: methyl ethanoate

☐ Since two reactants join up with the elimination of the atoms to make water, this kind of reaction is called a **condensation** reaction. The reaction is also referred to as **esterification**.

> *Do not confuse a condensation reaction with a **dehydration** reaction. Dehydration is the reverse of hydration. In a dehydration reaction, the atoms that are eliminated to make water come from the one molecule and there is no joining up of molecules.*

☐ The ' ⇌ ' sign shows that the making of an ester is a **reversible** reaction that can eventually reach **equilibrium** (see 'Equilibrium', page 115).

Breaking esters

☐ In the reverse of a condensation reaction, esters can be broken down to the alcohol and carboxylic acid by heating with an acid or an alkali.

☐ The ester always breaks in the middle of the molecule.

Example: *The breakdown of methyl propanoate*

$$CH_3-CH_2-C \overset{\displaystyle O}{\underset{\displaystyle O-CH_3}{\diagup\kern-0.5em\big\diagdown}} \qquad + \qquad H_2O$$

ester: methyl propanoate

$$\Updownarrow \quad \textbf{hydrolysis}$$

$$CH_3-CH_2-C \overset{\displaystyle O}{\underset{\displaystyle OH}{\diagup\kern-0.5em\diagdown}} \qquad + \qquad HO-CH_3$$

acid: propanoic acid   **alcohol: methanol**

☐ This kind of reaction is called a **hydrolysis** reaction (the breakdown of the ester to give smaller molecules occurs due to the addition of the atoms present in water).

> *Do not confuse a hydrolysis reaction with a **hydration** reaction. In a hydration reaction, the atoms from water are added to the one molecule and there is no splitting of molecules (see 'The alcohols', page 50).*

☐ The ' $\rightleftharpoons$ ' sign shows that the breakdown of an ester is also a reversible reaction that can eventually reach equilibrium.

Preparation in the lab

☐ Esters can be prepared in the lab by heating the alcohol and the carboxylic acid with concentrated sulphuric acid. The concentrated sulphuric acid acts as a catalyst for the reaction.

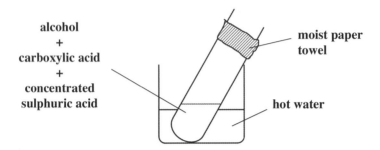

alcohol
+
carboxylic acid
+
concentrated
sulphuric acid

moist paper towel

hot water

☐ A moist paper towel at the top of the test tube acts as a condenser. The gases cool down, change back to a liquid and so reactants and products are retained in the test tube.

☐ A hot water bath is used rather than a Bunsen burner since the alcohol is flammable.

☐ The ester (insoluble in water) 'floats' on top of the water and can be recognised by the characteristic smell.

Uses of esters

☐ Esters evaporate relatively easily. This can lead to high concentrations of esters in the air. As a result, many uses of esters are based on their characteristic smells (see 'Volatile compounds', page 83),

  e.g. perfumes (attractive fragrance), artificial food flavourings (taste and smell are closely related).

☐ Esters are made up of relatively non-polar molecules. As a result, they are insoluble in water but are good solvents for many covalent compounds (see 'Properties of compounds', page 37),

  e.g. esters are used in paints, glues, varnishes and nail polish remover; ethyl ethanoate is used to clean electronic circuit boards.

3. FATS AND OILS

☐ Fats and oils can be classified as animal, vegetable or marine according to their origin.

☐ The main purpose of fats and oils in the diet is to provide energy. They are a more concentrated energy source than carbohydrates, i.e. they contain more energy per unit mass.

☐ Fats and oils are also essential for the transport and storage in the body of vitamins that are fat soluble/water insoluble.

☐ Fats and oils are examples of natural **esters**. They can be broken down to produce different carboxylic acids known as **fatty acids** and **glycerol**, an alcohol with three hydroxyl (-OH) groups per molecule.

☐ Fatty acids are carboxylic acids containing chains of even numbers of carbon atoms, ranging from C_4 to C_{24}, but usually chain lengths C_{16} or C_{18}.
The carbon chains of the fatty acids can be saturated or unsaturated,

   e.g. stearic acid, $C_{17}H_{35}COOH$ (saturated);

   oleic acid, $C_{17}H_{33}COOH$ (unsaturated).

☐ The saturated fatty acids all have the general formula $C_nH_{2n+1}COOH$.

☐ The systematic name for glycerol is propane-1,2,3-triol. The structure of glycerol is:

$$CH_2\!-\!OH$$
$$|$$
$$CH\ -\!OH$$
$$|$$
$$CH_2\!-\!OH$$

☐ An alcohol with three -OH groups is called a **triol**.

☐ An ester formed from glycerol is called a **triglyceride**.
Fats and oils consist largely of mixtures of triglycerides.

☐ In fats and oils, **three** moles of fatty acids are always combined with **one** mole of glycerol. The three fatty acid molecules combined with each molecule of glycerol may or may not be identical.

   | *R, R*, R** may or may not be the same carbon chain.* |

$$CH_2\!-\!O\!-\!\overset{\displaystyle O}{\overset{||}{C}}\!-\!R$$
$$|\qquad\ \ \overset{\displaystyle O}{}$$
$$CH\ -\!O\!-\!\overset{||}{C}\!-\!R^*$$
$$|\qquad\ \ \overset{\displaystyle O}{}$$
$$CH_2\!-\!O\!-\!\overset{||}{C}\!-\!R^{**}$$

☐ Since fats and oils are esters of long chain fatty acids and glycerol the breakdown of fats and oils during digestion produces fatty acids and glycerol in the ratio of three moles of fatty acid to one mole of glycerol.

| a fat or an oil | glycerol | fatty acid(s) |

☐ This process is an example of **hydrolysis**.

The melting points of fats and oils

☐ Fats and oils are mixtures of molecules some of which are saturated and some of which are unsaturated.

☐ In general, two differences between fats and oils are:

Fats	solid at 10 °C	more saturated molecules
Oils	liquid at 10 °C	more unsaturated molecules

☐ The lower melting points of oils compared with fats are related to the higher proportion of unsaturated molecules in oils.

☐ The saturated molecules are more closely packed. As a result, the Intermolecular forces of attraction (London dispersion forces) are relatively strong and so fats have relatively high melting points and are solid at room temperature.

☐ The shape of the unsaturated molecules in oils does not allow for close packing of the molecules. Consequently the intermolecular forces of attraction (London dispersion forces) are weaker and hence the melting points of oils are lower than that of fats.

☐ Oils can be **hardened** to make them more suitable for use as margarine. Removal of the unsaturation by the addition of hydrogen using a suitable catalyst raises the melting point. This is an example of a **hydrogenation** reaction.

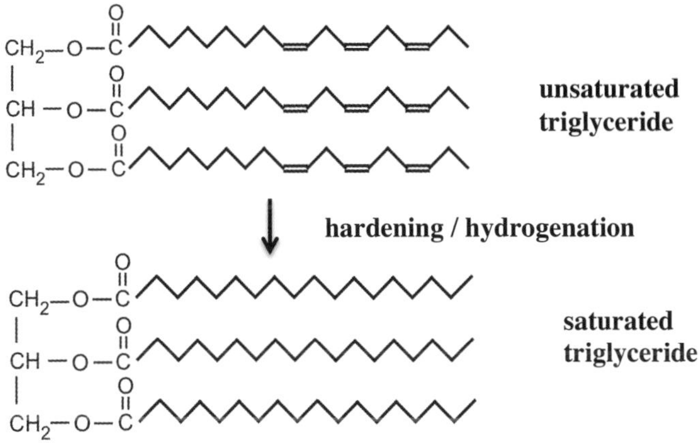

unsaturated
triglyceride

hardening / hydrogenation

saturated
triglyceride

Making soap

☐ Soaps are formed by the alkaline hydrolysis of fats and oils,

e.g. using sodium hydroxide.

☐ Since fats and oils are esters of long chain fatty acids and glycerol the breakdown of fats and oils produces fatty acids and glycerol in the ratio of three moles of fatty acid to one mole of glycerol (see 'Fats and oils', page 60).

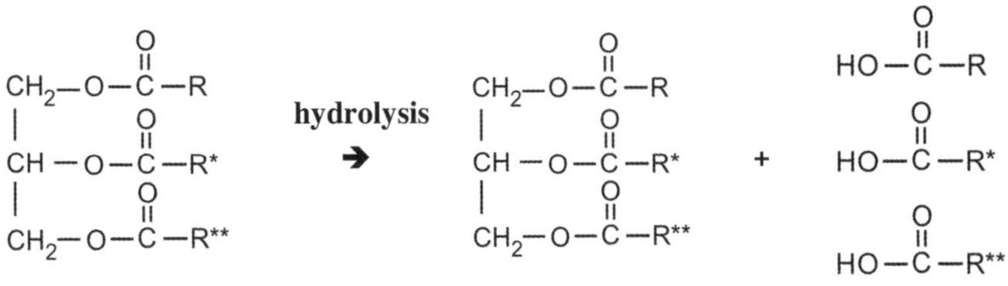

a fat or an oil   **glycerol**   **fatty acid(s)**

R, R*, R** *may or may not be the same long carbon chain.*

☐ This process is an example of **hydrolysis**.

☐ In alkaline conditions, the fatty acid molecules form ionic salts (and water) in a **neutralisation** reaction.

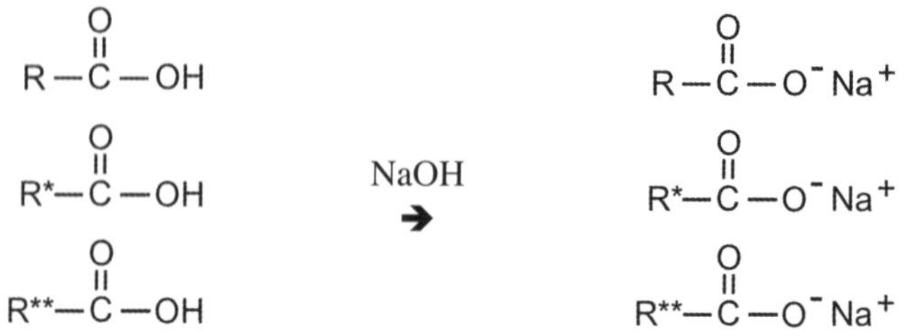

$$R-\underset{\underset{O}{\parallel}}{C}-OH$$

$$R^*-\underset{\underset{O}{\parallel}}{C}-OH \qquad \xrightarrow{\text{NaOH}} \qquad$$

$$R^{**}-\underset{\underset{O}{\parallel}}{C}-OH$$

fatty acid(s)

$$R-\underset{\underset{O}{\parallel}}{C}-O^-\,Na^+$$

$$R^*-\underset{\underset{O}{\parallel}}{C}-O^-\,Na^+$$

$$R^{**}-\underset{\underset{O}{\parallel}}{C}-O^-\,Na^+$$

salts(s)

☐ The sodium salts formed are water soluble and the main constituent of soaps.

Cleansing action of soaps

☐ Non-polar substances tend to be insoluble in water (see 'Properties of compounds', page 38). Cleaning with water alone has little effect on such 'stains',

e.g. water alone does not remove oil, grease or sweat from clothes.

☐ Soaps are ionic compounds. The negative ions have a long, non-polar, covalent carbon tail and an ionic carboxylate head (formed from a carboxylic acid). The positive ion comes from the alkali used in the hydrolysis of fats and oils.

$\text{\Large\bowtie\bowtie\bowtie\bowtie}$ COO⁻ Na⁺

covalent carbon tail   **ionic carboxylate head**

☐ The non-polar tail is **hydrophobic**, i.e. readily soluble in a non-polar substance; the ionic head is **hydrophilic**, i.e. soluble in water.

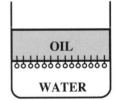

☐ During the cleaning of an oil stain, the hydrophobic tails dissolve in the non-polar oil and the hydrophilic heads dissolve in water.

☐ On shaking, the oil breaks up into tiny 'balls' with the hydrophilic heads facing out into the water.

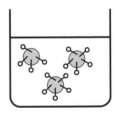

☐ The positive ions move into the water leaving a series of negative charges. This prevents the 'balls' coming together.

☐ Grease is removed from clothes in the same way.

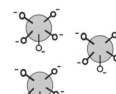

☐ An **emulsion** is a mixture of small droplets of one liquid dispersed in another liquid (or solution). The first liquid is insoluble in the second.

☐ The cleansing action of soap is based on the formation of an emulsion. The small droplets of oil are dispersed in the water.

Detergents

☐ In some parts of Scotland, the tap-water contains high concentrations of calcium ions (Ca^{2+}) and/or magnesium ions (Mg^{2+}).
This water is called **hard water**.

☐ Hard water forms a scum with soap instead of a lather. The scum is a result of the calcium ions and/or the magnesium ions reacting with the ionic head of the soap structure to form an insoluble salt.

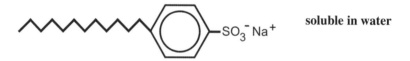

$$(\text{\textwidth}COO^-)_2 Ca^{2+}(s)$$

$$(\text{\textwidth}COO^-)_2 Mg^{2+}(s)$$

insoluble scum

☐ Chemists have produced a soap-like structure that does not react with calcium and/or magnesium ions to form an insoluble salt.

$$-SO_3^- Na^+$$ **soluble in water**

 is a representation for what is called a benzene ring.
This consists of a group of six carbon atoms and six hydrogen atoms.

☐ A cleaning product based on a compound with this structure is known as a **detergent**. The hydrophobic tail and hydrophilic head gives the structure the same cleansing action as a soap but the calcium and magnesium salts are soluble in water.

Emulsions in food

☐ Many foods consist of mixtures of oils and aqueous solutions,

    e.g. salad cream is mixtures of oils and vinegar.

☐ To form an emulsion and prevent the two components separating into layers, a molecule with a soap-like structure called an **emulsifier** is added,

    e.g. egg yolk is the emulsifier in salad cream.

☐ Many emulsifiers for use in a food product have a structure based on glycerol combined with long chain fatty acids but with only one of two fatty acids linked through ester groups rather than the three normally found in fats and oils.

$$
\begin{array}{ll}
& \quad\;\; O \\
& \quad\;\; \| \\
CH_2-O-C-R & \qquad\qquad CH_2-O-C-R \\
\quad\;\;\; O & \qquad\qquad\quad\; | \\
\quad\;\;\; \| & \\
CH-O-C-R^* & \qquad\qquad CH-OH \\
\quad\; | & \qquad\qquad\quad\; | \\
CH_2-OH & \qquad\qquad CH_2-OH
\end{array}
$$

☐ The one or two hydroxyl groups present in these molecules are polar (see 'Polar covalent bonds', page 23), making the molecule soluble in water (hydrophilic); the long carbon chains in the fatty acid part of the molecule are non-polar making the molecule soluble in non-polar compounds like oils (hydrophobic).

    covalent carbon tail: hydrophobic   **polar head: hydrophilic**

> *The* ▬ *represents the other arrangements of atoms in the various emulsifiers.*

☐ The action of an emulsifier can be compared with the cleansing action of soap. Both structures have a part that is hydrophobic and a part that is hydrophilic.

4. PROTEINS

☐ Proteins are an essential part of a balanced diet.

☐ They are the major structural materials of animal tissue,

   e.g. proteins are found in bones, muscle, body organs as well as skin and hair.

☐ They are also involved in cellular processes that are essential for the maintenance and regulation of life,

   e.g. the body uses proteins to make haemoglobin (the compound in red blood cells that carries oxygen).

Making proteins

☐ As well as carbon, hydrogen and oxygen, proteins contain **nitrogen.**

☐ The building blocks for proteins are **amino acid** molecules.

☐ Amino acids are relatively small molecules that all contain an amino (or amine) group ($-NH_2$) and a carboxylic acid (or carboxyl) group ($-COOH$).

☐ The structure of an amino acid molecule can be represented:

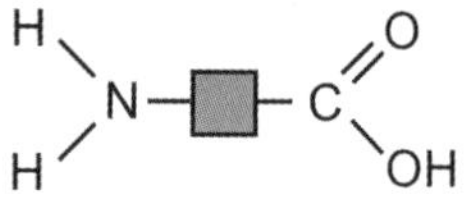

| **amino group** | **carboxyl group** |

The ▬■▬ *represents the other arrangements of atoms in the various amino acids.*

Examples

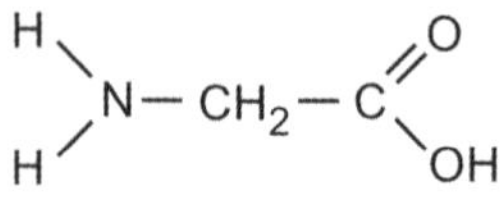

glycine

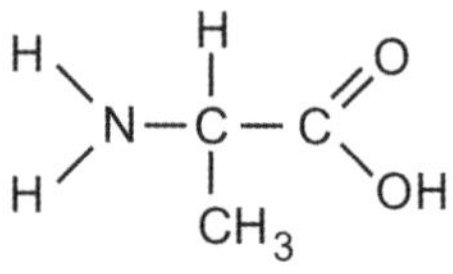

alanine

☐ Proteins are large polymer molecules made up of many amino acid molecules linked together. The carboxyl group and the amino group of neighbouring acid molecules can join together with the loss of the elements to form water.

condensation polymerisation ⬇

$$-N-\blacksquare-\overset{\overset{\displaystyle O}{\|}}{C}-N-\boxplus-\overset{\overset{\displaystyle O}{\|}}{C}-N-\diagup\!\!\!\diagup-\overset{\overset{\displaystyle O}{\|}}{C}- \quad + \quad H_2O$$

☐ A molecule consisting of two amino acid units joined together is called a **dipeptide**.

Example

glycine ⬇ **alanine**

☐ Since two molecules join up with the elimination of the elements to form water, the making of a protein is an example of **condensation polymerisation**.

> *Do not confuse a condensation reaction with a **dehydration** reaction. Dehydration is the reverse of hydration. In a dehydration reaction, the atoms that are eliminated to make water come from the one molecule and there is no joining up of molecules.*

☐ The $-\overset{\overset{\displaystyle O}{\|}}{C}-\overset{\overset{\displaystyle H}{|}}{N}-$ group that forms between the two amino acids is called a **peptide** (or an **amide**) link.

Breaking proteins

☐ In the reverse process, protein molecules are broken down with the addition of the elements from water to form amino acid molecules.

hydrolysis ⬇

☐ Since the breakdown of the protein to give smaller molecules occurs due to the addition of the elements from water, this is an example of a **hydrolysis** reaction.

> *Do not confuse a hydrolysis reaction with a **hydration** reaction. In a hydration reaction, the atoms from water are added to the one molecule and there is no splitting of molecules (see 'The alcohols', page 50).*

Reactions in the body

☐ Protein molecules have a very high molecular mass since the molecules consist of long chains often with several thousand amino acid molecules joined together.

☐ There are over 20 different amino acids found in proteins. The different possible sequences of these amino acids allow for the wide variety of different protein molecules. The different molecules have different roles in the body.

☐ During digestion, protein in food is hydrolysed into amino acids. These smaller molecules can be absorbed into the blood stream and taken to the various parts of the body to be reassembled in a different order to produce the actual proteins that the body requires.

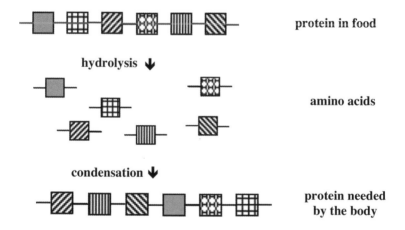

☐ Some of the amino acids required for body proteins can be made by the body. The body is dependent on dietary proteins (proteins in food) for the supply of amino acids that are required but cannot be made. These are known as **essential** amino acids.

Changes in shape

☐ Proteins are long chain molecules based on peptide links. The long chains may be twisted to form spirals, folded into sheets or wound around to form other complex shapes.

☐ The chains are held in these forms by **hydrogen bonding** (see 'Intermolecular forces', page 29). This bonding occurs between amino and carboxyl groups on side branches of the main polymer chain.

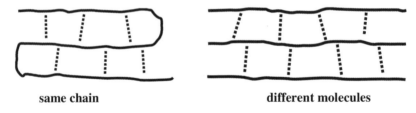

hydrogen bonding

☐ The hydrogen bonding can be within the same chain or between different molecules.

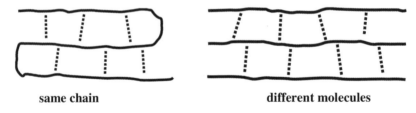

same chain   **different molecules**

☐ During cooking, when proteins are heated, the intermolecular bonds are broken and the protein changes shape. This process is called **denaturing**.

☐ Changes in the shapes of proteins alter the texture of foods,

e.g. during the cooking of an egg, the protein chains in the egg white unwind as the protein is denatured and new intermolecular bonds are formed across molecules in different chains causing the egg white to solidify.

☐ As well as changes in temperature, denaturing of proteins can also be a result of changes in pH.

Enzymes

☐ All **enzymes** are proteins. Enzymes are biological catalysts that speed up chemical reactions in living organisms,

 e.g. during digestion, pepsin is the enzyme involved in the hydrolysis of protein in foods to form amino acids.

☐ The shape of an enzyme molecule exactly complements the shape of the molecule upon which it acts. This allows the two molecules to briefly come together like a "lock-and-key", bringing about the reaction.

Example: A "building up" reaction

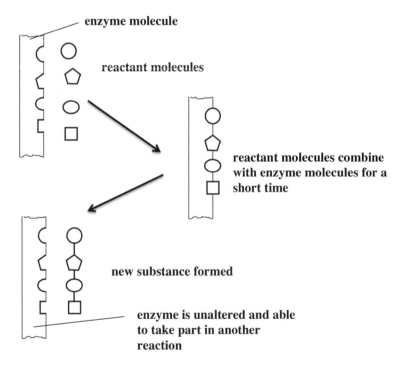

enzyme molecule

reactant molecules

reactant molecules combine with enzyme molecules for a short time

new substance formed

enzyme is unaltered and able to take part in another reaction

☐ Because of its specific shape, each enzyme is only able to promote one particular chemical reaction.

☐ The shape of protein molecules can be altered by changes in temperature and pH (denaturing) so that there is no longer a match with the particular reactants.

☐ Each enzyme works best at a particular temperature and pH. These are the **optimum conditions**.

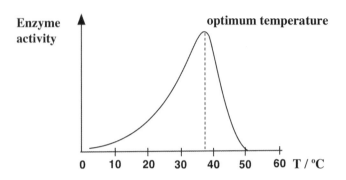

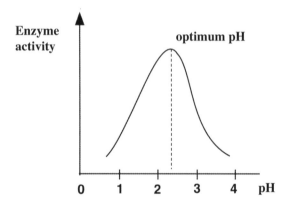

Polyamides

☐ Polyamides are synthetic fibres that consist of polymer molecules with amide links.

☐ **Kevlar** is formed by condensation polymerisation from two different monomer units.

molecule with carboxyl group at either end

molecule with amino group at either end

⬇ **condensation polymerisation**

☐ The repeating unit consists of two molecules linked together:

is a representation for what is called a benzene ring. This consists of a group of six carbon atoms and six hydrogen atoms.

- Kevlar is extremely strong because of the way that the rigid, linear molecules are packed together.

- Sheets of molecules are formed with the chains held together by **hydrogen bonds**. The sheets then stick together around the fibre axis to give an almost perfectly regular surface.

fibre axis

- **Nylon** is also a polyamide formed from two different monomer units. While one of the molecules also has an amino group at either end, in the other molecule the –OH of the carboxyl group has been replaced by a – Cl atom.

condensation polymerisation

- The repeating unit is:

- In the formation of nylon, hydrogen chloride molecules (rather than water molecules) are formed as the molecules link together to form the polymer. This reaction is also classed as an example of **condensation polymerisation**.

5. OXIDATION OF CARBON COMPOUNDS

Aldehydes and ketones

☐ Aldehydes and ketones are other examples of a homologous series.

☐ The functional group in an aldehyde and a ketone is the **carbonyl** group ($\diagdown$C=O).

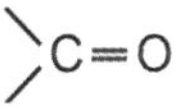

(a) Aldehydes

☐ In aldehydes the carbonyl group is always at the end of a carbon chain and so one of the bonds is linked to a hydrogen atom (there are two hydrogen atoms on either side of the carbonyl group in methanal).

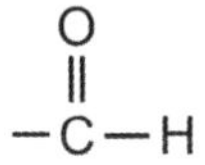

$$\begin{array}{c} O \\ \parallel \\ -C-H \end{array}$$

☐ Straight chain aldehydes take their name from the corresponding alkane. Each member has a name which ends in **-anal** and a prefix which indicates the number of carbon atoms in the molecule,

e.g. ethanal has the carbonyl group attached to one other carbon atom:

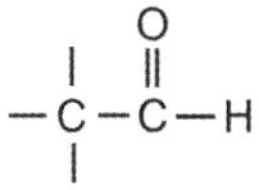

$$\begin{array}{c} \quad\;\; O \\ \mid \;\; \parallel \\ -C-C-H \\ \mid \end{array}$$

☐ The different ways of representing ethanal are shown below.

Full structural formula	Shortened structural formula	Formula
H O ‖ H−C−C ⟍ H	CH₃−C ⟍O / H or CH₃— CHO or CH₃CHO	C2H4O

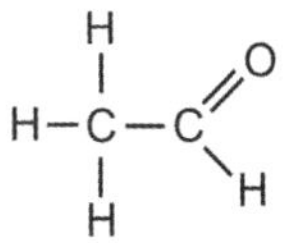

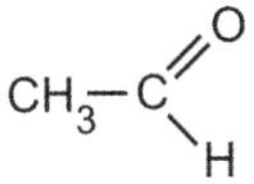

□ To name a branched-chain aldehyde:

1 Select the longest continuous chain of carbon atoms containing the carbonyl group and name it after the appropriate alkane.
2 Number the carbon atoms, starting from the end of the chain with the carbonyl group.
3 Name the branch(es) and indicate the position(s) of the branch(es) on the chain.

Examples

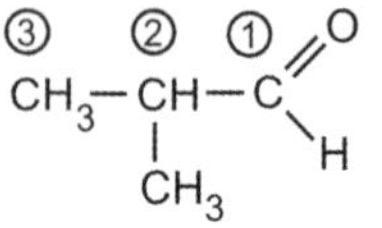

③ ② ①
CH_3-CH-C
    | O
   CH_3 H

methylpropanal

It is not necessary to number the methyl group in this case.

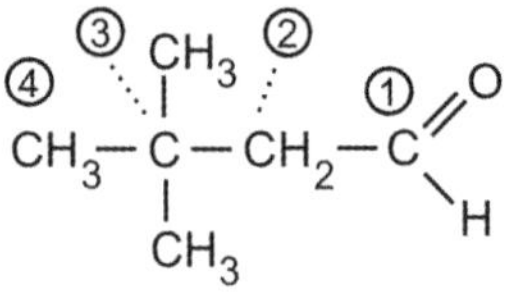

③ CH_3 ②
④ | ①
CH_3-C-CH_2-C
        | O
       CH_3 H

3,3-dimethylbutanal

(b) Ketones

☐ In ketones the carbonyl group is always in the middle of the carbon chain, i.e. linked to two other carbon atoms:

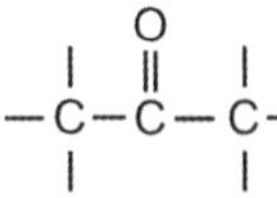

$$-\overset{|}{\underset{|}{C}}-\overset{O}{\overset{\|}{C}}-\overset{|}{\underset{|}{C}}-$$

☐ Straight chain ketones take their name from the corresponding alkane. Each member has a name which ends in **-anone** and a prefix which indicates the number of carbon atoms in the molecule.

☐ The different ways of representing propanone are shown below.

Full structural formula	Shortened structural formula	Formula
$$H-\overset{H}{\underset{H}{C}}-\overset{O}{\overset{\|}{C}}-\overset{H}{\underset{H}{C}}-H$$	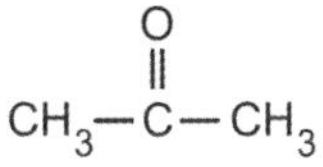 $$CH_3-\overset{O}{\overset{\|}{C}}-CH_3$$ or $$CH_3-CO-CH_3$$ or $$CH_3COCH_3$$	C_3H_6O

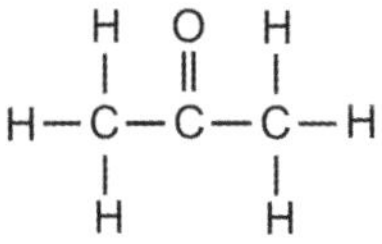

☐ From pentanone onwards, the carbonyl group can be in different positions in the carbon chain, giving rise to isomers.

Examples

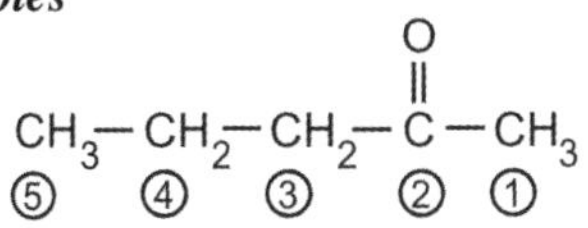

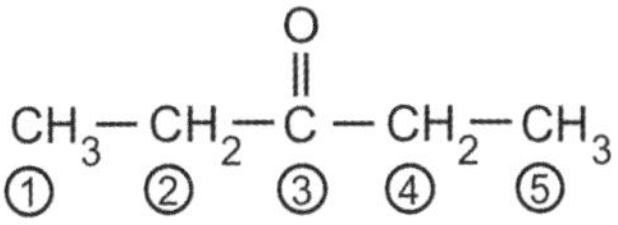

$$\underset{⑤}{CH_3}-\underset{④}{CH_2}-\underset{③}{CH_2}-\underset{②}{\overset{O}{\overset{\|}{C}}}-\underset{①}{CH_3}$$

$$\underset{①}{CH_3}-\underset{②}{CH_2}-\underset{③}{\overset{O}{\overset{\|}{C}}}-\underset{④}{CH_2}-\underset{⑤}{CH_3}$$

☐ To name a ketone:

1   Select the longest continuous chain of carbon atoms containing the carbonyl group and name it after the appropriate alkane.
2   Number the carbon atoms from the end of the chain nearer the carbonyl group and indicate the position of the carbonyl group.
3   Name any branch(es) and indicate the position(s) of the branch(es) on the carbon chain .

Examples

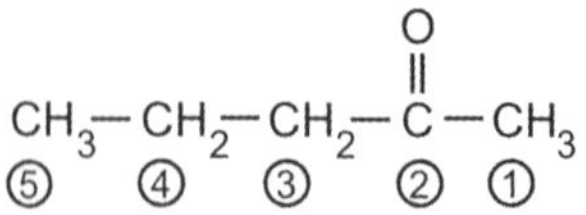

$$CH_3—CH_2—CH_2—\overset{\displaystyle O}{\overset{\|}{C}}—CH_3$$
⑤   ④   ③   ②   ①

pentan-2-one

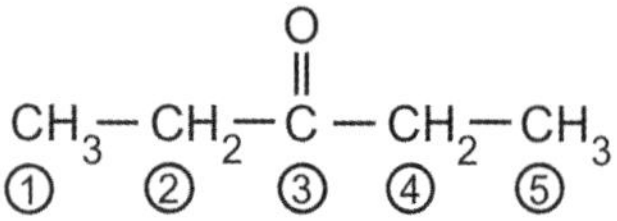

$$CH_3—CH_2—\overset{\displaystyle O}{\overset{\|}{C}}—CH_2—CH_3$$
①   ②   ③   ④   ⑤

pentan-3-one

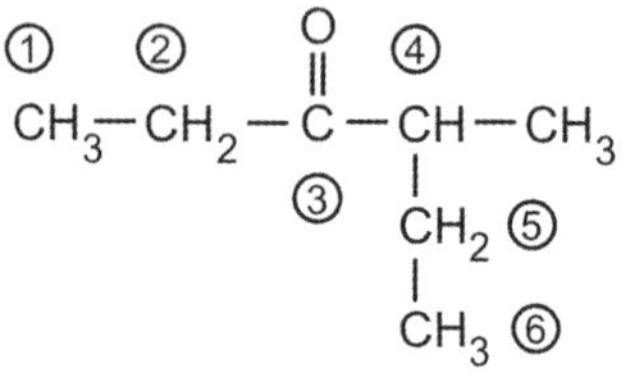

① ② $\overset{\displaystyle O}{\overset{\|}{C}}$ ④
$$CH_3—CH_2—C—CH—CH_3$$
③ $\underset{\displaystyle CH_3 \;⑥}{\underset{|}{\underset{\displaystyle CH_2 \;⑤}{\underset{|}{}}}}$

4-methylhexan-3-one

④   ③ $\overset{\displaystyle O}{\overset{\|}{}}$
$$CH_3—CH—C—CH_3$$
$\underset{\displaystyle CH_3}{\underset{|}{}}$ ② ①

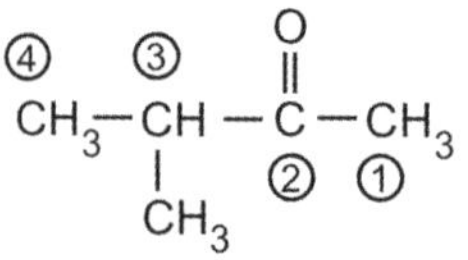

methylbutanone

It is not necessary to number the groups in this case.

Primary, secondary and tertiary alcohols

☐ To decide if an alcohol is primary, secondary or tertiary, look at the number of carbon atoms bonded to the carbon to which the hydroxyl group (-OH) is attached.

☐ **Primary** alcohol: **one** carbon atom attached to the carbon atom with the hydroxyl group (or none in the case of methanol); the hydroxyl group is always at the end of the chain.

$$\begin{array}{cc} H & H \\ | & | \\ -C-C-OH \\ | & | \\ H & \end{array}$$

☐ **Secondary** alcohol: **two** carbon atoms attached to the carbon atom with the hydroxyl group; the hydroxyl group is **not** at the end of a chain and there is **not** a branch on the same carbon as the group.

$$\begin{array}{ccc} H & H & H \\ | & | & | \\ -C-C-C- \\ | & | & | \\ & OH & \end{array}$$

☐ **Tertiary** alcohol: **three** carbon atoms attached to the carbon atom with the hydroxyl group; the hydroxyl group is **not** at the end of a chain and there is a branch on the same carbon as the group.

$$\begin{array}{ccc} & | & \\ & -C- & \\ | & | & | \\ -C-C-C- \\ | & | & | \\ & OH & \end{array}$$

Examples

propan-1-ol $CH_3-CH_2-CH_2-OH$ **primary**

propan-2-ol $CH_3-\overset{\displaystyle H}{\underset{\displaystyle OH}{C}}-CH_3$ **secondary**

2-methylbutan-2-ol $CH_3-CH_2-\overset{\displaystyle CH_3}{\underset{\displaystyle OH}{C}}-CH_3$ **tertiary**

Oxidation of alcohols

☐ Combustion (burning) is an oxidation process. Complete combustion takes place in a good supply of oxygen. For most alcohols, the products of complete combustion are carbon dioxide and water.

☐ **Primary** and **secondary** alcohols can undergo oxidation using an oxidising agent. The oxidising agent is reduced (see 'Oxidising and reducing agents', page 141).

☐ The (first) product of the oxidation of a primary alcohol is an **aldehyde**.

	primary alcohol	→	**aldehyde**
e.g.	*methanol*	→	*methanal*

☐ A secondary alcohol is oxidised to form a **ketone**.

	secondary alcohol	→	**ketone**
e.g.	*propan-2-ol*	→	*propanone*

☐ A tertiary alcohol is **not** oxidised in this way.

tertiary alcohol	→	**no reaction**

☐ **Acidified dichromate solution** is a suitable oxidising agent. The orange colour due to the dichromate ions changes to a blue-green colour due to the formation of chromium(III) ions in the reduction step.

$$Cr_2O_7^{2-} (aq) \ + \ 14H^+ (aq) \ + 6e^- \ \rightarrow \ 2Cr^{3+}(aq) \ + 7H_2O \ (l)$$

☐ Oxidation can also be achieved by passing the alcohol vapour over **hot copper(II) oxide** (black) which is reduced to copper (brown).

$$Cu^{2+}(s) \quad + \quad 2e^- \ \rightarrow \quad Cu(s)$$

Nature's Chemistry

☐ A primary alcohol but **not** a secondary alcohol can be further oxidised by a suitable oxidising agent to produce a **carboxylic acid** (see 'Oxidation of carbonyl compounds', page 82).

primary alcohol   ➔   aldehyde   ➔   carboxylic acid

e.g. methanol   ➔   *ethanal*   ➔   *ethanoic acid*

secondary alcohol   ➔   ketone   ⇏   no reaction

e.g. butan-2-ol   ➔   *butanone*

☐ Oxidation can be considered to be loss of hydrogen as well as gain of oxygen. Therefore, when applied to carbon compounds, oxidation results in an increase in the oxygen to hydrogen ratio.

☐ When applied to carbon compounds, the reverse reaction (reduction) results in a decrease in the oxygen to hydrogen ratio.

Oxidation of carbonyl compounds

☐ Aldehydes but **not** ketones can be readily oxidised by a suitable oxidising agent to produce a **carboxylic acid**.

aldehyde	→	carboxylic acid
e.g. ethanal	→	*ethanoic acid*
ketone	⇸	no reaction

☐ Suitable oxidising agents are:

Fehling's solution
Blue copper(II) ions in solution are reduced to form an orange-red precipitate of insoluble copper(I) oxide.

$$Cu^{2+}(aq) \quad + \quad e^- \quad \rightarrow \quad Cu^+(s)$$

Tollens' reagent
Silver ions are reduced to form a layer of silver metal on the wall of the glass container.

$$Ag^+(aq) \quad + \quad e^- \quad \rightarrow \quad Ag(s)$$

This is often referred to as the 'silver mirror test'.

Acidified dichromate solution
The orange colour due to the dichromate ions changes to a blue-green colour due to the formation of chromium(III) ions in the reduction step.

$$Cr_2O_7^{2-}(aq) \quad + \quad 14H^+(aq) \quad + \quad 6e^- \quad \rightarrow \quad 2Cr^{3+}(aq) \quad + \quad 7H_2O(l)$$

☐ A positive reaction with these solutions can be used to distinguish an aldehyde from a ketone.

6. EVERYDAY CHEMISTRY

Volatile compounds

☐ Detecting the flavour in foods is not just related to the sense of taste; the sense of smell is also important.

☐ Volatile compounds evaporate easily. Many of the flavours in food are due to the presence of volatile compounds with an aroma that can be detected by the nose.

☐ Many molecules with flavour and aroma are alcohols, aldehydes, ketones and esters,

e.g. *the diffusion of oxygen into whisky casks leads to the oxidation of the alcohol to produce the aldehydes that give distinctive flavours; esters are responsible for the aroma of many fruits and sweets.*

☐ The volatility of a covalent compound is related to:
- the mass of the molecule
- the functional group(s) in the molecule, i.e. the structure

☐ Differences in one of the above can only be use to explain differences in the volatility of a covalent compound if the other is kept as near constant as possible, i.e. in order to show the effect of increasing molecular mass, the structures should be kept the same. In order to show the effect of functional groups, the molecular mass should be kept the same.

Similar structure, different molecular mass

☐ For covalent compounds with similar structure, the volatility decreases with increasing molecular mass. This is due to the strength of the London dispersion forces increasing with increasing molecular mass (see 'Intermolecular forces', page 27).

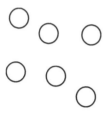

lower molecular mass

weaker intermolecular forces

easier to separate molecules

more volatile

higher molecular mass

stronger intermolecular forces

more difficult to separate molecules

less volatile

☐ Zingerone, $C_{11}H_{14}O_3$, puts the 'zing' in ginger. It has a similar molecular structure to vanillin, $C_8H_8O_3$. Vanillin has the aroma of vanilla. As a result of the higher molecular mass, zingerone can be predicted to be less volatile than vanillin.

zingerone

vanillin

Different structure, similar molecular mass

☐ The functional group in alcohols is the hydroxyl (-OH) group; the functional group in amines is the amino (-NH₂) group; the functional group in carboxylic acids is the carboxyl ($-C\overset{O}{\underset{OH}{\diagup}}$) group.

☐ The presence of these groups makes part of the molecule polar and tends to result in less volatile compounds compared with compounds of similar mass without the characteristic group.

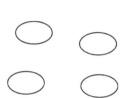

and / or

and / or

absence of functional group(s)	functional group(s) present
weaker intermolecular forces	stronger intermolecular forces (hydrogen bonding)
easier to separate molecules	more difficult to separate molecules
more volatile	less volatile

☐ Limonene, $C_{10}H_{16}$, is an unsaturated hydrocarbon.

Vanillin, $C_8H_8O_3$, has polar groups due to the oxygen atoms.

limonene

vanillin

 is a representation for what is called a benzene ring. This consists of a group of six carbon atoms and six hydrogen atoms.

☐ The significantly higher volatility of vanillin (although lower molecular mass) is due to the stronger intermolecular forces associated with the polar groups.

☐ The intermolecular forces in compounds with a hydroxyl group, an amino group or a carboxyl group are examples of hydrogen bonding (see 'Intermolecular bonding', page 29).

Soluble compounds

☐ Carbon compounds with molecules that have hydroxyl (-OH) and/or carboxyl (-COOH) groups have a polar part to the molecule and are likely to be soluble in water. Carbon compounds without these groups, likely to be non-polar, are less likely to be soluble in water but may be soluble in non-polar liquids (see 'Properties of compounds', page 37).

☐ Some foods have 'flavour compounds' that have polar groups in the molecules. Since these compounds are likely to be soluble in water, the foods should be cooked in oils/butter (mainly non-polar compounds) to retain the flavour molecules,

   e.g. asparagus.

☐ Foods with 'flavour compounds' that do not have polar groups in the molecules are likely to be more soluble in oils/butter (mainly non-polar compounds) than in water and so should be cooked in water,

   e.g. broccoli and green beans.

Essential oils

☐ **Essential oils** are volatile liquids with a strong aroma (fragrance or essence). The oils are mixtures of organic compounds and are insoluble in water (hydrophobic liquids).

☐ An oil is essential only in the sense that it carries the distinctive aroma of the plant.

☐ Essential oils are obtained by extraction from various parts of the plants,

   e.g. peel (orange and lemon), berry (juniper), leaf (basil and bay leaf) or flower (rose and lavender).

☐ Essential oils can be extracted from plants by steam distillation.

☐ They are widely used in perfumes, cosmetic products, cleaning products and as flavourings in foods.

☐ **Terpenes** are the key components of most essential oils.
They are unsaturated hydrocarbons that are formed by joining together units of isoprene (2–methylbuta–1,3–diene), formula C_5H_8.

The full structural formula for isoprene is shown:

isoprene

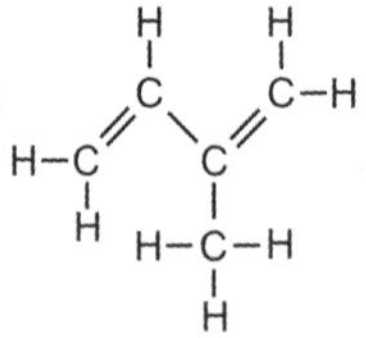

☐ The basic molecular formula for terpenes is $(C_5H_8)_n$ where n is the number of units in the terpene.

☐ Terpenes can be classified as follows.

	Isoprene units	Carbon atoms
monoterpene	2	C_{10}
diterpene	4	C_{20}
triterpene	6	C_{30}

☐ As well as being linked together 'head to tail' to form linear chains, the isoprene units can be arranged to form rings,

*e.g.   myrcene, found in thyme and other plants, is a linear monoterpene;
limonene, found in lemon peel and other citrus fruits, is a cyclic
monoterpene.*

myrcene

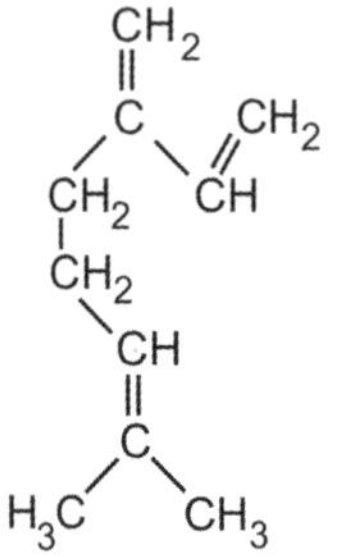

limonene

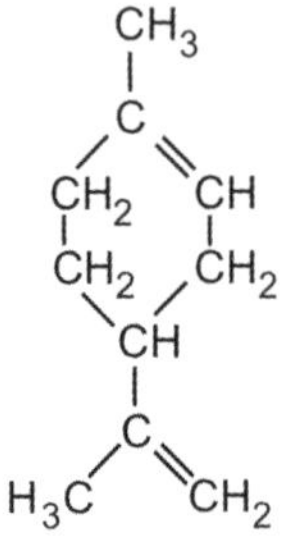

☐ Terpenes can be oxidised within plants producing a range of compounds (called terpenoids) responsible for distinctive aromas,

e.g. the oxidation of terpenes is responsible for the distinctive flavours of spices such as cloves, cinnamon and ginger.

☐ The oxidised terpene can have alcohol, aldehyde or ketone functional groups,

e.g. terpineol is an alcohol commonly used in perfumes and cosmetics.

terpineol

Antioxidants

☐ Oxidation is a chemical reaction that involves loss of electrons; reduction is a chemical reaction that involves gain of electrons (see 'Oxidation and reduction', page 138).

☐ Exposure to oxygen can lead to the oxidation of molecules in foods. Such oxidation reactions can damage cells and lead to the deterioration of flavour, decrease in nutritional value, loss of colour and health risks from oxidation products,

   e.g. oxygen reacts with edible oils giving food a rancid flavour; in fruits such as apples, oxidation can result in the formation of compounds that discolour the fruit.

☐ Some foods are packaged to prevent oxidation,

   e.g. crisps are packaged with nitrogen, cucumbers are sealed in cellophane or coated in wax.

☐ **Antioxidants** inhibit the oxidation of molecules in foods. They are added to extend shelf-life and to help preserve quality,

   e..g vitamin C (ascorbic acid) is used an antioxidant.

☐ Antioxidants are themselves oxidised, so antioxidants are reducing agents (see 'Oxidising and reducing agents', page 141).

☐ Ion-electron equations can be written for the oxidation of antioxidants.

   Example: vitamin C (ascorbic acid)

   $$C_6H_8O_6 \text{ (aq)} \quad \rightarrow \quad C_6H_6O_6 \text{ (aq)} \quad + \quad 2H^+ \text{ (aq)} \quad + \quad 2e^-$$

☐ A standard solution of iodine can be used to determine by titration the mass of vitamin C in fruit juice. The iodine is oxidised to iodide ions (see 'Redox titrations', page 152).

   $$I_2 \text{ (aq)} \quad + \quad 2e^- \quad \rightarrow \quad 2I^- \text{ (aq)}$$

Free radicals

☐ **Free radicals** are atoms or groups of atoms with one or more unpaired electrons,

  e.g. a chlorine atom, $Cl^\bullet$, a methyl group, $CH_3^\bullet$.

  | The 'dot $^\bullet$' represents the unpaired electron. |

☐ Due to the unpaired electrons, free radicals are very reactive and can cause significant damage to cells within the body.

☐ Ultraviolet (UV) radiation is a high energy form of light, present in sunlight. The formation of free radicals is a result of molecules gaining sufficient energy for bonds to be broken.

☐ While short term exposure can cause sunburn, prolonged exposure to UV light over a person's lifetime can damage the skin due to the formation of free radicals, a process that is known as **photoaging**. Sun-block products limit the damage by producing a barrier to UV radiation reaching the skin.

☐ **Free radical scavengers** are molecules that are very reactive. They 'mop up' other free radicals to form stable molecules and thus prevent the damaging reactions.

☐ Many cosmetics products contain free radical scavengers,

  e.g. anti-aging creams.

☐ Some oxidation reactions involve free radicals; free radical scavengers can be added to products to reduce deterioration due to oxidation,

  e.g. free radical scavengers are added to food products and plastics.

☐ Free radical scavengers that reduce damage by oxidation processes involving free radicals are also known as antioxidants (see 'Antioxidants', page 90),

  e.g. vitamin C (ascorbic acid) is a free radical scavenger added to foods.

☐ Free radical scavengers can occur naturally,

  e.g. vitamin E can help to prevent free radical damage to cells in the body.

Free radical chain reactions

☐ A free radical chain reaction is one that continues because for every free radical that is produced at the beginning, a similar new free radical is generated at the end. Each one includes the following steps: initiation, propagation and termination.

☐ In the **initiation** step the chain is started by UV light breaking covalent bonds to form free radicals. The chain **propagation** reactions, in which a reacting free radical is also a product, are the ones that keep the chain going. In the chain **termination** step, free radicals are removed when two collide and join together without producing any new free radicals and so the reaction eventually stops.

☐ The reaction is referred to as a **chain reaction** since one of the products of the propagation steps is also a reactant.

(a) The reaction of an alkane with bromine

☐ An alkane, e.g. hexane, will decolourise bromine faster in light than in dark. In the initiation step the light energy breaks the bromine–bromine covalent bonds producing bromine free radicals.

initiation step

$$Br_2 \quad \rightarrow \quad Br^{\bullet} \quad + \quad Br^{\bullet}$$

☐ The propagation steps involve the reaction of bromine free radicals with hexane molecules to form hydrocarbon free radicals and hydrogen bromide molecules. The hydrocarbon free radicals can then react with bromine molecules to produce bromohexane and bromine free radicals.

propagation steps

$$Br^{\bullet} \quad + \quad C_6H_{14} \quad \rightarrow \quad C_6H_{13}^{\bullet} \quad + \quad HBr$$

$$C_6H_{13}^{\bullet} \quad + \quad Br_2 \quad \rightarrow \quad C_6H_{13}Br \quad + \quad Br^{\bullet}$$

- The bromine free radical, one of the reactants, is also a product of the propagation reactions.

- The termination steps involve the reaction of free radicals with free radicals. Without free radicals the reaction stops.

termination steps

$$Br^{\bullet} \quad + \quad Br^{\bullet} \quad \rightarrow \quad Br_2$$

$$Br^{\bullet} \quad + \quad C_6H_{13}^{\bullet} \quad \rightarrow \quad C_6H_{13}Br$$

$$C_6H_{13}^{\bullet} \quad + \quad C_6H_{13}^{\bullet} \quad \rightarrow \quad C_{12}H_{26}$$

(b) The reaction of hydrogen and chlorine

- Hydrogen reacts explosively with chlorine in a free radical chain reaction that is initiated by light, e.g. light from burning magnesium or a photographic flash unit.

initiation step

$$Cl_2 \quad \rightarrow \quad Cl^{\bullet} \quad + \quad Cl^{\bullet}$$

propagation steps

$$Cl^{\bullet} \quad + \quad H_2 \quad \rightarrow \quad HCl \quad + \quad H^{\bullet}$$

$$H^{\bullet} \quad + \quad Cl_2 \quad \rightarrow \quad HCl \quad + \quad Cl^{\bullet}$$

termination steps

$$Cl^{\bullet} \quad + \quad Cl^{\bullet} \quad \rightarrow \quad Cl_2$$

$$H^{\bullet} \quad + \quad H^{\bullet} \quad \rightarrow \quad H_2$$

$$H^{\bullet} \quad + \quad Cl^{\bullet} \quad \rightarrow \quad HCl$$

Unit 3   Principles to Production

1. THE DESIGN OF AN INDUSTRIAL PROCESS

☐   As well as making a major impact on the quality of our lives, the UK chemical industry makes a significant contribution to the national economy.

☐   Industrial processes are designed to maximise profit and minimise the damaging impact on the environment; often there has to be a compromise between the two.

☐   The reactants from which other chemicals can be extracted or synthesised are known as **feedstocks**.

☐   Factors that influence the design of an industrial process include

* the **availability** and **cost** of the feedstock(s),

> *e.g. the gases of the air, water and minerals such as salt (sodium chloride) and limestone (calcium carbonate) are all raw materials that are readily available and relatively cheap; fossil fuels such as oil and gas are likely to be more costly to obtain and there are competing demands for use of these raw materials for the chemical industry with their use for fuels.*

* the **sustainability** (future availability) of the feedstock(s),

> *e.g. air and water are not going to run out in the same way as fossil fuels.*

* the opportunity to **recycle** unused reactant(s) (economically advantageous)

> *e.g. in the manufacture of ammonia by the Haber Process, the unreacted nitrogen and hydrogen are recycled.*

* the **energy requirements**,

> *e.g. the energy released in exothermic reactions can be used to raise the temperature of reactants and hence reduce energy costs.*

* the formation of **marketable by-products** (that can be sold to reduce costs),

> *e.g. hydrogen, which can be used as a fuel, is produced as a by-product in the cracking of ethane and the reforming of naphtha; sulphur, found in fossil fuels, is removed during the distillation of crude oil for use as a feedstock in the manufacture of sulphuric acid.*

* **the rate of production**,

> *e.g. the cost of increasing temperature and/or the use of an expensive catalyst to increase the reaction rate and hence yield of product in a fixed time has to be balanced against the cost of energy/the catalyst and may actually reduce profits.*

Example: The Solvay Process

The manufacture of sodium carbonate by this process is economical because two of the products of reactions (ammonium chloride and carbon dioxide) are **recycled** and the feedstocks (limestone, coke, air and sea water) are all relatively **available** and **cheap** to obtain.

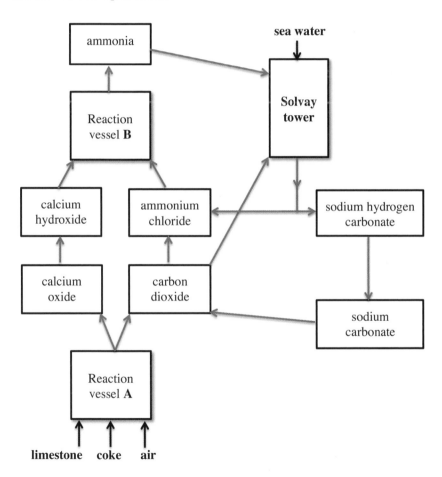

☐ Environmental issues are also of major importance:

* the discharge of harmful chemicals has been greatly reduced,

    e.g. the concentration of acids and alkalis in factory effluents is carefully controlled; the removal of the sulphur in fossil fuels reduces levels of sulphur dioxide in the atmosphere.

* waste is minimised (see atom economy),

    e.g. in the manufacture of ammonia (recycling), the cracking of ethane (hydrogen is a useful useful by-product), a new process for the manufacture of ibuprofen (fewer steps and so likely to be more efficient).

* the use and production of toxic substances tend to be avoided,

    e.g. the use of organochlorine compounds has now been phased out due to their toxicity to animals; they also produce toxic fumes when burned.

* biodegradable products are designed if appropriate,

    e.g. the use of biodegradable plastics made from plants avoid the problems caused by non-biodegradable plastics which are usually made from oil; the use of starch based plastics allows microorganisms to break the plastics down to carbon dioxide.

2. CHEMICAL CALCULATIONS

The mole (revision)

☐ One **mole** (symbol mol) of any substance is defined as the formula mass in grams, i.e. the gram formula mass (GFM).

☐ The formula mass is obtained from the formula by adding together all the relative atomic masses of the atoms (or ions).

☐ To calculate the mass of one mole of the substance, simply change the units to grams.

Example 1: Calculate the mass of one mole of sodium.

Step 1	Formula	Na
Step 2	Find the relative atomic mass	23
Step 3	Change units to grams	**23 g**

Example 2: Calculate the mass of one mole of calcium hydroxide.

Step 1   Formula $Ca(OH)_2$

Step 2   Find the relative atomic masses

	Ca	O	H
	40	16	1

Step 3   Multiply by the number
         of atoms   40   16 x 2   1   x   2

> *Note that the brackets mean that the 2 refers to both the oxygen and hydrogen.*

Step 4   Do the sum   40   +   32   +   2

Step 5   Formula mass   74

Step 6   Change units to grams   **74 g**

Example 3:   Calculate the mass of two moles of sodium chloride.

Step 1	Formula		NaCl

Step 2	Find the relative atomic masses	Na	Cl
		23	35.5

Step 3   Multiply by the number   23 x 1   35.5 x 1
         of atoms

Step 4   Do the sum   23   +   35.5

Step 5   Formula mass   58.5

Step 6   Change units to grams (GFM)   58.5 g

Step 7   Complete calculation   mass =   no. of moles x GFM

$$\boxed{m = n \times GFM}$$

$$= \ 2 \times 58.5$$

$$= \ \textbf{117 g}$$

Example 4:   Calculate the number of moles in 36 g of water.

Step 1   Formula H_2O

Step 2   Find the relative atomic masses   H   O
                                            1   16

Step 3   Multiply by the number   1 x 2   16 x 1
         of atoms

Step 4   Do the sum   2   +   16

Step 5   Formula mass   18

Step 6   Change units to grams (GFM)   18 g

Step 7   Complete calculation   no. of moles = $\dfrac{mass}{GFM}$

$$\boxed{n = \frac{m}{GFM}}$$

$$= \ \frac{36}{18}$$

$$= \ \textbf{2 mol}$$

Using concentration (revision)

- [ ] The concentration of an aqueous solution is expressed as the mass of substance dissolved in a certain volume of water.

- [ ] The concentration can be expressed as grams per litre, g l^{-1}; this can also be written as g/l.

- [ ] The concentration is often expressed in terms of the number of moles of substance dissolved in water to make 1 litre of solution, i.e. mol l^{-1} (or mol/l).

- [ ] A solution labelled 1 mol l^{-1} contains **one** mole of substance dissolved in water and made up to one litre of solution; a solution labelled 2 mol l^{-1} contains **two** moles of substance dissolved in water and made up to one litre of solution.

Example 1: **Calculate the number of moles of sodium hydroxide in 100 cm^3 solution, concentration 0.4 mol l^{-1}.**

$$n = CV$$

no. of moles	=	conc x litres
	=	0.4 x 0.1
	=	**0.04 mol**

Example 2: **Calculate the concentration of a solution of hydrochloric acid containing 0.1 mol in 50 cm^3.**

$$C = \frac{n}{V}$$

conc	=	$\dfrac{\text{no. of moles}}{\text{litres}}$
	=	$\dfrac{0.1}{0.05}$
	=	**2 mol l^{-1}**

Example 3: **Calculate the volume of a sodium carbonate solution, concentration 2 mol l^{-1}, that contains 0.5 mol.**

$$V = \frac{n}{C}$$

litres	=	$\dfrac{\text{no. of moles}}{\text{conc}}$
	=	$\dfrac{0.5}{2}$
	=	**0.25 l (250 cm^3)**

Example 4: **Calculate the concentration of a solution containing 2 g sodium hydroxide in 50 cm^3 solution.**

Step 1   Formula   NaOH

Step 2   Mass of one mole (GFM) $23 + 16 + 1 = 40$ g

Step 3   Number of moles   no. of moles $= \dfrac{\text{mass}}{\text{GFM}}$

$$\boxed{n = \dfrac{m}{\text{GFM}}}$$

$$= \dfrac{2}{40}$$

$$= 0.05 \text{ mol}$$

Step 4   Complete calculation   conc $= \dfrac{\text{no. of moles}}{\text{litres}}$

$$\boxed{C = \dfrac{n}{V}}$$

$$= \dfrac{0.05}{0.05}$$

$$= \mathbf{1 \ mol \ l^{-1}}$$

Example 5: **Calculate the mass of calcium chloride in 25 cm^3 of a solution, concentration 0.1 mol l^{-1}.**

Step 1   Number of moles   no. of moles $=$ conc x litres

$$\boxed{n = C \times V}$$

$$= 0.1 \times 0.025$$

$$= 0.0025$$

Step 2   Formula $CaCl_2$

Step 3   Mass of one mole (GFM) $40 + (2 \times 35.5) = 111$ g

Step 4   Complete calculation   mass $=$ no. of moles x GFM

$$\boxed{m = n \times \text{GFM}}$$

$$= 0.0025 \times 111$$

$$= \mathbf{0.2775 \ g}$$

The Avogadro Constant (i)

☐ One mole of any substance contains the same number of 'elementary entities' as there are atoms in exactly 12 g of carbon-12.

☐ Elementary entities may be atoms, molecules, ions, electrons or other particles.

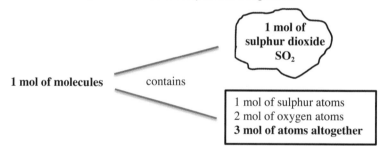

one mole	one mole	one mole	one mole
12 g of carbon-12	**23 g of sodium**	**18 g of water**	**100 g of calcium carbonate**
the same number of C **atoms**	the same number of Na **atoms**	the same number of H_2O **molecules**	the same number of $CaCO_3$ **units**

☐ Molecules are made up of atoms covalently bonded together.

1 mol of molecules   contains

> **1 mol of sulphur dioxide SO_2**

> 1 mol of sulphur atoms
> 2 mol of oxygen atoms
> **3 mol of atoms altogether**

☐ Ionic compounds are made up of oppositely charged ions held together by forces of attraction.

1 mol of formula units   contains

> **1 mol of calcium bromide $CaBr_2$**

> 1 mol of calcium ions
> 2 mol of bromide ions
> **3 mol of ions altogether**

☐ The actual number of elementary entities per mole is known as the **Avogadro Constant**, (symbol L).

☐ The Avogadro Constant $= 6.02 \times 10^{23}\,mol^{-1}$

☐ For elements with a formula that is just the chemical symbol, the chemical units are atoms.

Examples

1 mol of copper, Cu, contains 6.02×10^{23} Cu atoms.

0.5 mol of argon, Ar, contains 3.01×10^{23} Ar atoms.

☐ For covalently bonded elements and compounds the chemical units are molecules.

Examples

1 mol of water, H_2O, contains 6.02×10^{23} H_2O molecules.

0.1 mol of methane, CH_4, contains 6.02×10^{22} CH_4 molecules.

☐ For ionic compounds the chemical units are formula units.

Examples

1 mol of magnesium chloride, $MgCl_2$,
contains 6.02×10^{23} $MgCl_2$ formula units.

2 mol of sodium sulphate, Na_2SO_4,
contains 1.204×10^{24} Na_2SO_4 formula units.

Example 1:   Which contains more atoms, 6 g of carbon or 6 g of sodium?

1 mol of carbon   i.e. GFM $= 12$ g

$$n = \frac{m}{GFM}$$ no. of moles $= \dfrac{6}{12} = 0.5$ mol

1 mol of sodium   i.e. GFM $= 23$ g

no. of moles $= \dfrac{6}{23} = 0.26$ mol

6 g of carbon has a greater number of moles and hence contains more atoms.

Example 2:   Which contains more molecules, 36 g of water or 44 g of carbon dioxide?

1 mol of water (H_2O), i.e. GFM = 18 g

$$\boxed{n = \frac{m}{GFM}}$$

no. of moles $= \dfrac{36}{18} = 2$ mol

1 mol of carbon dioxide (CO_2), i.e. GFM = 44 g

36 g of water has a greater number of moles and hence contains more molecules.

Example 3:   Which contains more ions, 6.2 g of sodium oxide or 10.11 g of potassium nitrate?

1 mol of sodium oxide (Na_2O), i.e. GFM = 62 g

$$\boxed{n = \frac{m}{GFM}}$$

no. of moles $= \dfrac{6.2}{62} = 0.1$ mol

Each Na_2O unit contains **three** ions, i.e. two Na^+ and one O^{2-}.

1 mol of potassium nitrate (KNO_3), i.e. GFM = 101.1 g

no. of moles $= \dfrac{10.11}{101.1} = 0.1$ mol

Each KNO_3 unit contains **two** ions, i.e. one K^+ and one NO_3^-.

0.1 mol of Na_2O contains 0.3 mol of ions,
whereas 0.1 mol of KNO_3 contains 0.2 mol of ions.

Example 4: Which contains more atoms, 9 g of water or 6.4 g of methane?

1 mol of water (H_2O), i.e. GFM = 18 g

$$\boxed{n = \frac{m}{GFM}}$$ no. of moles $= \frac{9}{18} = 0.5$ mol

Each molecule of H_2O unit contains **three** atoms, i.e. two H and one O.

1 mol of methane (CH_4), i.e. GFM = 16 g

no. of moles $= \frac{6.4}{16} = 0.4$ mol

Each molecule of CH_4 unit contains **five** atoms, i.e. one C and four H.

9 g of water contains 1.5 mol of atoms (3 x 0.5),
whereas **6.4 g of methane** contains 2 mol of atoms (5 x 0.4).

The Avogadro Constant (ii)

> *The following examples are **not** part of the mandatory content of the course. However, given the Avogadro Constant, you could perhaps meet calculations of this kind in a problem-solving context.*

Example 1:   How many atoms are in 0.6 g of carbon?

1 mol of carbon   =   12 g

12 g (1 mol)   ⟵——————⟶ 6×10^{23} atoms

0.6 g   ⟵——————⟶ $6 \times 10^{23} \times \dfrac{0.6}{12}$

                             =   **3×10^{22} atoms**

Example 2:   How many molecules in 3.2×10^{-3} g methane?

1 mol of methane (CH_4)   =   16 g

16 g (1 mol)   ⟵——————⟶ 6×10^{23} molecules

3.2×10^{-3} g   ⟵——————⟶ $6 \times 10^{23} \times \dfrac{3.2 \times 10^{-3}}{16}$

                             =   **1.2×10^{20} molecules**

Example 3:   How many ions in 1g of calcium carbonate?

1 mol of calcium carbonate   =   100 g

100 g (1 mol)   ⟵——————⟶ 6×10^{23} $CaCO_3$ units

1 g   ⟵——————⟶ $6 \times 10^{23} \times \dfrac{1}{100}$

                             = 6×10^{21} $CaCO_3$ units

Each $CaCO_3$ unit contains **two** ions, i.e. one Ca^{2+} and one CO_3^{2-}, so... 1 g contains $2 \times 6 \times 10^{21}$ ions = **1.2×10^{22} ions**

Molar volume of gases

□ The molar volume of a gas is the volume occupied by one mole. The molar volume is dependent on the temperature and the pressure of the gas. The unit of molar volume is litres mol^{-1}.

Example 1: **Calculate the mass of 2 litres of methane.**

(Take the molar volume of methane to be 22.4 litres mol^{-1}.)

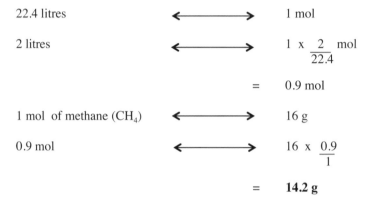

22.4 litres   ⟷   1 mol

2 litres   ⟷ $1 \times \dfrac{2}{22.4}$ mol

      =   0.9 mol

1 mol of methane (CH_4)   ⟷   16 g

0.9 mol   ⟷ $16 \times \dfrac{0.9}{1}$

      =   **14.2 g**

Example 2: A 1 litre flask contained 2.82 g of sulphur dioxide.

Calculate the molar volume of the gas (at the particular temperature and pressure).

1 mol of sulphur dioxide (SO_2) = 64 g

$$\boxed{n = \dfrac{m}{GFM}}$$

$$\text{no. of moles} = \dfrac{\text{Mass}}{GFM}$$

$$= \dfrac{2.82}{64}$$

$$= 0.044$$

0.044 mol   ⟷   1 litre

1 mol   ⟷ $1 \times \dfrac{1}{0.044}$

      =   **22.7 litres**

Calculations based on equations (i) (revision)

☐ A balanced equation gives information about the relative quantities involved in the reaction. This is expressed in terms of the relative number of moles of each reactant and product.

☐ Since the mass of one mole of any substance is the formula mass in grams, the masses involved can then be calculated.

Example 1: **Calculate the mass of water produced on burning 1 g of methane.**

Step 1 Balanced equation $\quad CH_4 \; + \; 2O_2 \quad \longrightarrow \quad CO_2 \; + \; 2H_2O$

Step 2 Relative number $\quad$ 1 mol $\qquad\qquad\qquad\qquad\qquad$ 2 mol
$\quad$ of moles

> *It is not necessary to calculate the masses of carbon dioxide and oxygen as these substances are not included in the question.*

Step 3 Find the formula masses $\qquad CH_4 \qquad\qquad H_2O$

$\qquad\qquad 12 + (1 \times 4) \qquad (1 \times 2) + 16$

$\qquad\qquad\qquad = 16 \qquad\qquad = 18$

Step 4 Mass in grams $\qquad\qquad 16$ g $\qquad\qquad 18$ g

Step 5 Multiply by the number $\qquad 16$ g $\qquad\qquad 2 \times 18$ g
$\quad$ of moles

$\qquad\qquad\qquad\qquad\qquad\qquad = 36$ g

Step 6 Complete calculation $\qquad 16$ g $\longleftrightarrow$ 36 g

$\qquad\qquad\qquad\qquad\quad 1$ g $\longleftrightarrow$ $36 \times \dfrac{1}{16}$

$\qquad\qquad\qquad\qquad\qquad\qquad = \mathbf{2.25}$ **g**

Example 2: An industrial plant produces ammonia, NH_3, from nitrogen and hydrogen. An output of 7.5×10^3 kg of ammonia is required each day.

Calculate the daily mass of nitrogen needed for this output to be achieved.

Step 1 Balanced equation

$$N_2 \quad + \quad 3H_2 \quad \longrightarrow \quad 2NH_3$$

Step 2 Relative number of moles

1 mol   2 mol

Step 3 Find the formula masses

14 x 2   14 + (1 x 3)

= 28   = 17

Step 4 Mass in grams

28 g   17 g

Step 5 Multiply by the number of moles

28 g   2 x 17 g

= 34 g

Step 6 Complete calculation

28 g $\longleftrightarrow$ 34 g

$28 \times \dfrac{7.5 \times 10^3}{34}$ $\longleftrightarrow$ 7.5×10^3

$$= \mathbf{6.18 \times 10^3 \ kg}$$

There is no need to change kg into g in this kind of calculation.
The unit in the answer will always be the same as the unit given in the question ... this could be g, kg or even tonnes.
In the example above, the question indicates an output of 7.5×10^3 kg and this is used in the calculation in step 6, hence the answer is in kg.

Chemistry in Society

Calculations based on equations (ii)

☐ When doing experiments with gases it is much more convenient to measure volumes than masses.

Example 1: **Calculate the volume of carbon dioxide produced by the complete combustion of 7 g of ethene, C_2H_4.**

(Take the molar volume of methane to be 22.0 litres mol^{-1}.)

Balanced equation

$$C_2H_4 \quad + \quad 3O_2 \quad \rightarrow \quad 2CO_2 \quad + \quad 2H_2O$$

1 mol   2 mol

28 g (1 mol)   ⟵⟶   2 x 22 litres

7 g   ⟵⟶ $2 \times 22 \times \dfrac{7}{28}$

= **11 litres**

Example 2: **Calculate the volume of hydrogen produced when excess zinc reacts with 25 cm^3 of hydrochloric acid, concentration 0.1 mol l^{-1}.**

(Take the molar volume of hydrogen to be 22.2 litres mol^{-1}.)

$$\boxed{n = CV}$$ no. of moles of HCl (aq)   =   conc x litres

=   0.1 x 0.025

=   0.0025 mol

Balanced equation

$$Zn \quad + \quad 2HCl \,(aq) \quad \rightarrow \quad ZnCl_2 \quad + \quad H_2$$

2 mol   ⟵⟶   1 mol (22.2 litres)

0.0025 mol   ⟵⟶ $22.2 \times \dfrac{0.0025}{2}$

=   **0.0278 litres (27.8 cm^3)**

The idea of excess

☐ All reactants are needed for a chemical reaction to take place. When one of the reactants is used up the reaction will stop. Any reactant which is left unreacted is said to be "in excess".

Example 1: 8g of methane (CH_4) is mixed with 16 g of oxygen.
A spark is applied to the mixture to start the reaction.

Calculate the mass of carbon dioxide produced.

Balanced equation CH_4 + $2O_2$ → CO_2 + $2H_2O$

Relative number
of moles   1 mol   2 mol   1 mol

$$\boxed{n = \frac{m}{GFM}}$$ methane   no. of moles $= \dfrac{m}{GFM} = \dfrac{8}{16} = 0.5$ mol

oxygen   no. of moles $= \dfrac{m}{GFM} = \dfrac{16}{32} = 0.5$ mol

Which reactant is in excess?

From the balanced equation,   1 mol of CH_4 reacts with 2 mol of O_2

0.25 mol of CH_4 reacts with 0.5 mol of O_2

Since there is 0.5 mol of CH_4, **CH_4 is in excess**.

Which reactant controls the mass of products?

Methane is in excess; the oxygen will all be used up;
the mass of products will depend on the number of moles of oxygen.

Complete calculation

2 mol O_2 ⟵——————⟶   1 mol CO_2

64 g   ⟵——————⟶   44 g

16 g   ⟵——————⟶   **11 g**

Example 2: What mass of hydrogen gas is produced when 4.86 g of magnesium is added to 100 cm^3 of dilute hydrochloric acid, concentration 1 mol l^{-1}?

Balanced equation   Mg   +   2HCl (aq)   →   MgCl$_2$ +   H$_2$

Relative number   1 mol   2 mol   1 mol
of moles

$$n = \frac{m}{GFM}$$

no. of moles of magnesium $= \frac{m}{GFM} = \frac{4.86}{24.3} = 0.2$ mol

$$n = CV$$

no. of moles of HCl (aq)   =   conc x litres

                                    =   1 x 0.1

                                    =   0.1 mol

Which reactant is in excess?

From the balanced equation,   1 mol of Mg reacts with 2 mol of HCl (aq)

0.05 mol of Mg reacts with 0.1 mol of HCl (aq)

Since there is 0.2 mol of Mg, **Mg is in excess.**

Which reactant controls the mass of products?

Magnesium is in excess; the acid will all be used up;
the mass of products will depend on the number of moles of acid.

Complete calculation

2 mol HCl (aq)   ←——————→   1 mol H$_2$

2 mol   ←——————→   2 g

0.1 mol   ←——————→   **0.1 g**

Calculations based on equations (iii)

☐ One mole of any gas contains the same number of molecules (or atoms in the case of the noble gases) and occupies the same volume (at the same temperature and pressure).

☐ This means that equal volumes of gases contain the same number of moles.

1 litre of O_2 (g)	1 litre of H_2 (g)	1 litre of CO_2 (g)	1 litre of Ar (g)

same number of moles

☐ The balanced equation gives the relative number of moles of reactants and products.

Example	N_2 (g)	+	$3H_2$ (g)	➜	$2NH_3$ (g)
	1 mol		3 mol		2 mol
so ...	1 litre	+	3 litre	➜	2 litre
or ...	$10 \, cm^3$	+	$30 \, cm^3$	➜	$20 \, cm^3$
or ...	$1 \, cm^3$	+	$3 \, cm^3$	➜	$2 \, cm^3$

In the above reaction the volume of the product is half the volume of the reactants.

☐ Liquid or solid reactants and products have negligible volumes compared to gases and their volumes can be ignored in this type of calculation.

Example	C (s)	+	O_2 (g)	➜	CO_2 (g)
	1 mol		1 mol		1 mol
so ...	not a gas		1 litre	➜	1 litre
or ...			$10 \, cm^3$	➜	$10 \, cm^3$
or ...			$1 \, cm^3$	➜	$1 \, cm^3$

In this reaction the volume of the product is equal to the volume of the reactant.

Example 1: **What volume of oxygen is required for 50 cm^3 of hydrogen to completely burn to produce water?**

Balanced equation $2H_2$ (g)   + O_2 (g)   → $2H_2O$ (l)

                      2 mol   1 mol

    so...   50 cm^3 requires   **25 cm^3**

Example 2:   70 cm^3 of ethene, C_2H_4, is completely burned in excess of oxygen.

    (a) **What is the volume and composition of the gas at the end of the experiment at 20 °C?**

    (b) **What would be the volume if the experiment was repeated at 120 °C?**

(a)

Balanced equation

        C_2H_4 (g)   + $3O_2$ (g)   → $2CO_2$ (g)   + $2H_2O$ (l)

        1 mol   excess   2 mol

  so... 70 cm^3 **140 cm^3**

Water is **not** a gas at 20 °C so the volume of water can be ignored.

(b)

Water is a gas at 120 °C so the volume is included.

        C_2H_4 (g)   + $3O_2$ (g)   → $2CO_2$ (g)   + $2H_2O$(g)

        1 mol   excess   2 mol   2 mol

  so... 70 cm^3 140 cm^3 +   140 cm^3

                          total   **280 cm^3**

Example 3: 30 cm³ of methane is completely burned in 100 cm³ of oxygen.

What is the volume and composition of the gas at the end of the experiment at 20 ºC?

balanced equation

$$CH_4\,(g) \quad + \quad 2O_2\,(g) \quad \rightarrow \quad CO_2\,(g) \quad + \quad 2H_2O\,(l)$$

1 mol   2 mol   1 mol   (not a gas)

Which reactant is in excess?

From the balanced equation,

    1 mol of CH_4 2 mol of $2O_2$

so ... 30 cm³   60 cm³

Since there is 100 cm³ of O_2, **O_2 is in excess**.

Which reactant controls the volume of products?

Oxygen is in excess; the methane will all be used up;
the volume of products will depend on the volume of methane.

Complete calculation

$$CH_4\,(g) \quad + \quad 2O_2\,(g) \quad \rightarrow \quad CO_2\,(g) \quad + \quad 2H_2O\,(l)$$

1 mol   2 mol   1 mol   (not a gas)

30 cm³   60 cm³   30 cm³   (not a gas)

    Volumes that react   Volume that is produced

Volumes of gases at the end of experiment

    O_2 (unreacted)   =   **40 cm³**   (100 cm³ - 60 cm³)

    CO_2 (produced)   =   **30 cm³**

3. EQUILIBRIUM

Dynamic equilibrium

☐ Many reactions are reversible; the forward and backward reactions occur at the same time and the reaction mixture contains both reactants and products.

☐ If the external conditions are not altered a balance point will be reached and the reaction will appear to have stopped; at this point the reaction has attained a state of **dynamic equilibrium.**

☐ At equilibrium the rates of the forward and backward reactions are equal.

☐ At equilibrium **the concentrations of the reactants and the products will remain constant** but are unlikely to be equal.

☐ The sign ' $\rightleftharpoons$ ' is used to show that a reaction is at equilibrium.

Example

$$A \quad + \quad B \quad \rightleftharpoons \quad C \quad + \quad D$$

☐ At equilibrium, if the concentrations of **A** and **B** are less than those of **C** and **D**, the equilibrium position lies to the right, i.e. to the side of the products.

☐ For such a reaction, the changes in the concentrations of reactants and products as equilibrium is established can be illustrated:

start $A \quad + \quad B \longrightarrow$

$A \quad + \quad B \rightleftharpoons C + D$

$A \quad + \quad B \rightleftharpoons C \quad + \quad D$

equilibrium $A \quad + \quad B \rightleftharpoons C \quad + \quad D$

☐ At equilibrium, if the concentrations of **A** and **B** are greater than **C** and **D** the equilibrium position lies to the left, i.e. to the side of the reactants.

☐ The equilibrium position is the same regardless of whether it is approached from the reactant or product side.

Factors which effect the position of equilibrium

(a) Concentration

☐ Addition of reactant or removal of product will increase the rate of the forward reaction compared to the backward reaction. This will cause the equilibrium to shift to the right (product side). At the new equilibrium position the concentration of products will be higher.

☐ Addition of product or removal of reactant will decrease the rate of the forward reaction compared to the backward reaction. This will cause the equilibrium to shift to the left (reactant side). At the new equilibrium position the concentration of reactants will be higher.

Example $Fe^{3+}(aq)$ + $SCN^-(aq)$ $\rightleftharpoons$ $FeSCN^{2+}(aq)$

Change in concentration	Direction in which equilibrium moves
$Fe^{3+}(aq)$ increase	to the right
$FeSCN^{2+}(aq)$ increase	to the left
$SCN^-(aq)$ decrease	to the left

☐ The removal of a reactant or product can be a result of a reaction with the chemical added.

Example
$$Cl_2(aq) \quad + \quad H_2O(l) \quad \rightleftharpoons \quad ClO^-(aq) \quad + \quad Cl^-(aq)$$

The addition of silver nitrate solution, $AgNO_3$ (aq), will remove Cl^- (aq) ions. The reaction produces a precipitate of silver chloride, $AgCl$ (s). As a result the equilibrium will move to the right.

(b) Temperature

☐ Increasing the temperature will increase the rate of both reactions but the one that removes heat will be favoured, i.e. the equilibrium will shift in the endothermic direction.

☐ Decreasing the temperature will decrease the rate of both reactions but the one that produces heat is not reduced as much, i.e. the equilibrium will shift in the exothermic direction.

Example N_2O_4 (g) $\rightleftharpoons$ $2NO_2$ (g) ΔH +ve

Change in temperature	Direction in which equilibrium moves
increase	to the right
decrease	to the left

(c) Pressure

☐ Increasing the pressure will increase the rate of reaction that reduces the number of gaseous molecules.

☐ Decreasing the pressure will increase the rate of reaction that increases the number of gaseous molecules.

Example N_2O_4 (g) $\rightleftharpoons$ $2NO_2$ (g)

Change in pressure	Direction in which equilibrium moves
increase	to the left
decrease	to the right

☐ If the number of moles of gaseous reactant is equal to the number of moles of gaseous product, the equilibrium is unaffected by changes in pressure.

Example H_2 (g)   + Cl_2 (g) $\rightleftharpoons$ $2HCl$ (g)

☐ A reaction involving gas(es) will only attain equilibrium if it is carried out in a closed container. If the container is open then the gas(es) will constantly escape reducing the concentration of the gas(es).

Example $\quad CaCO_3 (s) \quad \rightleftharpoons \quad CaO (s) \quad + \quad CO_2 (g)$

The decomposition of calcium carbonate will only attain equilibrium in a closed container. In an open container, $CO_2 (g)$ will escape and the equilibrium will continue to shift to the right until all $CaCO_3$ has decomposed.

An alternative approach

☐ When one of the factors that affects the position of equilibrium is changed, the equilibrium will shift in the direction that 'opposes' the change.

(a) Concentration

☐ When a reactant is added to (or a product removed from) an equilibrium, the equilibrium will shift to oppose that change, i.e. remove the added reactant or add the removed product.

$$\text{Reactant(s)} \quad \xrightarrow{\hspace{2cm}} \rightleftharpoons \quad \text{Product(s)}$$

The equilibrium will therefore shift to the right.

☐ When a product is added to (or a reactant removed from) an equilibrium, the equilibrium will shift to oppose that change, i.e. remove the added product or add the removed reactant.

$$\text{Reactant(s)} \quad \xleftarrow{\hspace{2cm}} \rightleftharpoons \quad \text{Product(s)}$$

The equilibrium will therefore shift to the left.

(b) Temperature

☐ An exothermic reaction gives out energy. The reaction can be thought of as:

$$\text{Reactant(s)} \quad \longrightarrow \quad \text{Product(s)} \quad + \quad \text{'ENERGY'}$$

☐ An endothermic reaction takes in energy. The reaction can be thought of as:

$$\text{Reactant(s)} \quad + \quad \text{'ENERGY'} \quad \longrightarrow \quad \text{Product(s)}$$

☐ An increase in temperature can be thought of as adding energy to the equilibrium. The equilibrium will shift to oppose the change, i.e. the reaction that takes in 'ENERGY', the endothermic reaction, will be favoured.

☐ A decrease in temperature can be thought of as removing energy from the equilibrium. The equilibrium will shift to oppose the change, i.e. the reaction that gives out 'ENERGY', the exothermic reaction, will be favoured.

(c) Pressure

☐ To oppose an increase in pressure, the equilibrium will shift in the direction that decreases the pressure, i.e. in the direction with the fewer number of moles of gas.

☐ To oppose a decrease in pressure, the equilibrium will shift in the direction that increases the pressure, i.e. in the direction with the greater number of moles of gas.

The effect of a catalyst

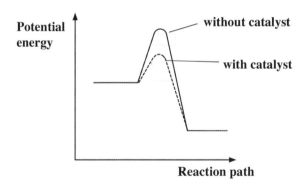

☐ If a catalyst is added there is the same decrease in the activation energies of the forward and backward reactions and the rates of both the forward and backward reactions will be increased.

☐ A catalyst, therefore, does **not** alter the position of equilibrium, i.e. a catalyst does not increase the percentage conversion of reactants into products

☐ Although a catalyst does not alter the equilibrium position, it does speed up the rate of attainment of equilibrium.

Equilibrium in industry: The industrial manufacture of ammonia by the Haber Process

☐ To maximise profits, industrial chemists employ strategies to move the position of the equilibrium in favour of increasing the yield of products.

☐ Conditions are carefully chosen to provide a compromise between a fast production, a high yield and low costs.

☐ The reaction of nitrogen and hydrogen to produce ammonia is reversible and if the conditions were kept constant, equilibrium would be attained.

$$N_2 (g) \quad + \quad 3H_2 (g) \quad \rightleftharpoons \quad 2NH_3 (g) \quad \Delta H = -91 \text{ kJ mol}^{-1}$$

(a) Concentration

☐ The Haber Process does not actually ever attain equilibrium. In a condenser, the ammonia gas is cooled and the liquid ammonia piped off. Constantly removing the ammonia gas decreases the rate of the backward reaction.

☐ In addition, the unreacted nitrogen gas and hydrogen gas are recycled. The increase in the concentrations of the reactant gases increases the rate of the forward reaction.

(b) Pressure

☐ Since the number of product molecules is less than the number of reactant molecules, increasing the pressure increases the rate of the forward reaction compared to the backward reaction. The pressure chosen is about 200 atmospheres. Beyond this pressure, the relative increase in the rate of the forward reaction can not justify the increased production costs.

(c) Temperature

☐ Since the reaction is exothermic, increasing the temperature favours the backward reaction. Increasing the temperature also increases the rate of both the forward and backward reactions and so it takes less time to reach the equilibrium position. In order to compromise, the Haber Process is carried out at a moderately high temperature of about 400 °C.

(d)   Use of a catalyst

☐ Using a catalyst increases the rates of both the forward and backward reactions. Although the yield is unaffected, it takes less time to reach the equilibrium position. This allows the process to be carried out more efficiently at a lower temperature.

4. PERCENTAGE YIELD AND THE ATOM ECONOMY

☐ The efficiency with which reactants are converted into the desired product can be measured in terms of the **percentage yield** and the **atom economy**; these are important considerations for industrial chemists.

☐ When calculating the percentage yield and the atom economy, the equations for the reactions **must be balanced**.

(a) Percentage yield

☐ The **actual yield** in a chemical reaction is the quantity of desired product that is formed for a particular set of reaction conditions.

☐ The **theoretical yield** is the quantity of desired product that is obtained, assuming full conversion of the limiting reactant (the one not in excess), as calculated from the balanced equation.

☐ The **percentage yield** gives a measure of the extent to which the limiting reactant is converted into the desired product.

☐ The percentage yield can be calculated from the equation:

$$\text{Percentage yield} = \frac{\text{Actual yield}}{\text{Theoretical yield}} \times 100$$

☐ The percentage yield is an important consideration for industrial chemists.

Example 1: 5 g of methanol reacts with excess ethanoic acid to produce 9.6 g of methyl ethanoate.

Calculate the percentage yield.

Method 1

Balanced equation

$$CH_3OH \quad + \quad CH_3COOH \quad \rightleftharpoons \quad CH_3OOCCH_3$$

1 mol		1 mol
32 g	$\longleftrightarrow$	74 g
5 g	$\longleftrightarrow$	$74 \times \dfrac{5}{32}$ g
		$= \quad 11.56$ g

Theoretical yield $\quad = \quad$ 11.56 g

Actual yield $\qquad = \quad$ 9.6 g

Percentage yield $\quad = \quad \dfrac{\text{Actual yield}}{\text{Theoretical yield}} = \dfrac{9.6}{11.56} \text{ x } 100 = \textbf{83\%}$

Method 2

$$\boxed{n = \frac{m}{GFM}}$$ no. of moles of methanol, $CH_3OH \quad = \quad \dfrac{5}{32} = 0.156$ mol

no. of moles of methyl methanoate, $CH_3OOCCH_3 \quad = \quad \dfrac{9.6}{74} = 0.130$ mol

Balanced equation

$$CH_3OH \quad + \quad CH_3COOH \quad \rightleftharpoons \quad CH_3OOCCH_3$$

1 mol		1 mol
0.156 mol	$\longleftrightarrow$	0.156 mol

Theoretical yield $\quad = \quad$ 0.156 mol

Actual yield $\qquad = \quad$ 0.130 mol

Percentage yield $\quad = \quad \dfrac{\text{Actual yield}}{\text{Theoretical yield}} \text{ x } 100 = \dfrac{0.130}{0.156} \text{ x } 100 = \textbf{83\%}$

Example 2: Under test conditions, 10 kg of nitrogen reacts with excess hydrogen to produce 1 kg of ammonia.

Calculate the percentage yield.

Method 1

Balanced equation $\qquad$ $N_2(g)$ $\qquad$ + $\qquad$ $3H_2(g)$ $\qquad$ $\rightleftharpoons$ $\qquad$ $2NH_3(g)$

There is no need to	1 mol
change kg to g in	28 g ←—→
this type of	
calculation. The	10 kg ←—→
unit in the answer is	
always the same as	
the unit in the step.	

$\qquad\qquad\qquad\qquad\qquad\qquad$ 2 mol

$\qquad\qquad\qquad\qquad\qquad\qquad$ 2 x 17 g

$\qquad\qquad\qquad\qquad\qquad\qquad$ 34 x $\dfrac{10}{28}$

$\qquad\qquad\qquad\qquad\qquad\qquad$ = 12.14 kg

Theoretical yield $\qquad$ = $\qquad$ 12.14 kg

Actual yield $\qquad$ = $\qquad$ 1 kg

Percentage yield $\qquad$ = $\qquad$ $\dfrac{\text{Actual yield}}{\text{Theoretical yield}}$ $\quad$ = $\dfrac{1}{12.14}$ x 100 = **8.2%**

Method 2

Express ratio of masses in grams $\qquad$ 10 kg nitrogen ←—→ 1 kg ammonia

$\qquad\qquad\qquad\qquad\qquad\qquad\qquad\qquad$ 10 g nitrogen ←—→ 1 g ammonia

$\boxed{n = \dfrac{m}{\text{GFM}}}$ $\qquad$ no. of moles of nitrogen $\quad$ = $\quad$ $\dfrac{10}{28}$ $\quad$ = $\quad$ 0.36 mol

$\qquad\qquad\qquad\qquad$ no. of moles of ammonia $\quad$ = $\quad$ $\dfrac{1}{17}$ $\quad$ = $\quad$ 0.059 mol

Balanced equation $\quad$ $N_2(g)$ $\qquad$ + $\qquad$ $3H_2(g)$ $\qquad$ $\rightleftharpoons$ $\qquad$ $2NH_3(g)$

$\qquad\qquad\qquad\qquad\quad$ 1 mol $\qquad\qquad\qquad\qquad\qquad\qquad\qquad\qquad$ 2 mol

$\qquad\qquad\qquad\qquad\quad$ 0.36 mol $\quad$ ←—→ $\qquad\qquad\qquad\qquad$ 0.72 mol

Theoretical yield $\quad$ = $\qquad$ 0.72 mol

Actual yield $\qquad$ = $\qquad$ 0.059 mol

Percentage yield $\quad$ = $\qquad$ $\dfrac{\text{Actual yield}}{\text{Theoretical yield}}$ x 100 $\quad$ = $\quad$ $\dfrac{0.059}{0.72}$ x 100 $\quad$ = **8.2%**

(b) Atom economy

☐ In an ideal chemical reaction, the total mass of all reactants is successfully converted into the desired product; this means there is no waste.

☐ The proportion of the total mass that is successfully converted is known as the atom economy; there is no waste in a reaction with an atom economy of 100%.

☐ The atom economy can be calculated from the equation:

$$\text{Atom economy} = \frac{\text{Mass of desired product(s)}}{\text{Total mass of reactants}} \times 100$$

Example 1: Sulphur dioxide combines with oxygen to form sulphur trioxide.
Calculate the atom economy for the reaction.

Balanced equation	$2SO_2$	+	O_2	→	$2SO_3$
	2 mol		1 mol		2 mol
	2 x 64 g		32 g		2 x 80 g
	128 g		32 g		160 g

$$\text{Atom economy} = \frac{\text{Mass of desired product } (SO_3)}{\text{Total mass of reactants}} \times 100$$

$$= \frac{160}{160} \times 100 = \textbf{100 \%}$$

☐ In terms of atom economy, a reaction with one product is completely efficient, i.e. there is no waste.

Example

Any reaction of the type: **A**   +   **B**   →   **X**

Example 2: Hydrogen can be made by reacting coal (carbon) with steam. Carbon dioxide is a by-product.

Calculate the atom economy for the reaction.

Balanced equation	C	+	$2H_2O$	$\rightarrow$	$2H_2$	+	CO_2
	1 mol		2 mol		1 mol		2 mol
	12 g		2 x 18 g		2 x 2 g		
	12 g		36 g		4 g		

$$\text{Atom economy} = \frac{\text{Mass of desired product }(H_2)}{\text{Total mass of reactants}} \times 100$$

$$= \frac{4}{48} \times 100 = \textbf{8.3 \%}$$

☐ In terms of atom economy, the process is an inefficient way to make hydrogen.

☐ Reactions that have a high percentage yield may have a low atom economy value if large quantities of unwanted by-products are formed.

☐ Increasing the atom economy for a reaction means that there is less waste to dispose of and so can be considered to be a 'greener' way of making the desired product,

  e.g. the method to manufacture ibuprofen was changed in the 1980's to increase the atom economy for the reaction used.

☐ The high costs and finite nature of raw materials (such as petrochemical reactants) have increased sensitivity to environmental concerns and also made atom economy considerations more relevant.

5. CHEMICAL ENERGY

Enthalpy of combustion

☐ The change in chemical energy of a reaction (the **enthalpy change, ΔH**) can be calculated from the specific heat capacity, mass and temperature change.

☐ The **enthalpy of combustion** of a substance is the heat given out when one mole of the substance burns completely in oxygen.

Example: **Use the results below to calculate the enthalpy of combustion of ethanol.**

$$C_2H_5OH \text{ (l)} \quad + \quad 3O_2 \text{ (g)} \quad \rightarrow \quad 3H_2O \text{ (g)} \quad + \quad 2CO_2 \text{ (g)}$$

Mass of burner at start	=	80.63 g
Mass of burner at end	=	80.48 g
Temperature of water at start	=	20.5 °C
Temperature of water at end	=	30.5 °C
Volume of water	=	100 cm^3

Calculation

Mass of ethanol used	=	0.15 g
Rise in temperature	=	10 °C

> *It is assumed that the heat that is given out by the burning ethanol is taken in by the water in the container, e.g. a copper can.*

Heat released   =   c m ΔT

$E_h = c \, m \, \Delta T$			
	=	4.18 x 0.1 x 10	=	4.18 kJ

c	=	specific heat capacity of water	=	4.18 kJ kg^{-1} °C^{-1}
m	=	mass of water absorbing heat in kilograms (1 cm^3 of water has a mass of 0.01 kg)		
ΔT	=	temperature change		

Chemistry in Society

Mass of one mole of ethanol (CH_3CH_2OH) = 46 g

Heat released per mole of ethanol

0.15 g of ethanol ⟷ 4.18 kJ

46 g (1 mol) ⟷ $4.18 \times \dfrac{46}{0.15}$

= **1282 kJ**

Enthalpy of combustion of ethanol is **-1282 kJ mol⁻¹**.
(The sign is negative to indicate an exothermic reaction.)

☐ Enthalpies of combustion can often be directly measured using a calorimeter and values for common compounds are available from data books for use in Hess's Law calculations (see 'Hess's Law', page 128).

☐ The lab. experimental values are less than the data book values because it is assumed that all the heat energy from the burning is gained by the water. Energy is however lost to the copper can and the surrounding air.

☐ The enthalpies of combustion of some organic compounds are found on page 10 of the Data Booklet.

Example: The first three members of the homologous series of alcohols

Alcohol	Structural formula	Enthalpy of combustion / kJ mol⁻¹
methanol	CH_3OH	-726
ethanol	CH_3CH_2OH	-1367
propan-1-ol	$CH_3CH_2CH_2OH$	-2021

☐ There is a fairly constant difference between the enthalpies of combustion for any two successive members of a homologous series. Since each pair differ by a $-CH_2-$ group the bond breaking energy and energy of bond making with oxygen is approximately constant for this group in different molecules,

  e.g. the enthalpy of combustion of butan-1-ol can be predicted to be approximately 2667 kJ mol⁻¹.

Hess's Law

☐ The law of conservation of energy states that energy can neither be created nor destroyed.

☐ The application of the law of conservation of energy to chemical reactions is known as Hess's Law.

☐ Hess's Law states that the enthalpy change in converting reactants into products is the same regardless of the route by which the reaction takes place.

Example: *The reaction* A ➔ B
may proceed by the three different routes.

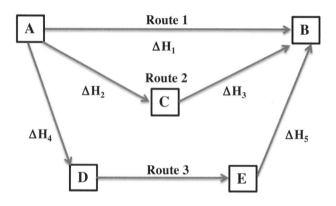

Total enthalpy change for Route 1   = ΔH_1
Total enthalpy change for Route 2   = ΔH_2 + ΔH_3
Total enthalpy change for Route 3   = ΔH_4 + ΔH_5 + ΔH_6

According to Hess's Law the total enthalpy change for Routes 1, 2 and 3 will be identical,
i.e. ΔH_1 = ΔH_2 + ΔH_3
              = ΔH_4 + ΔH_5 + ΔH_6

Example 1: Calculate the enthalpy change for the reaction:

$$RbCl\ (s) \rightarrow Rb^+\ (g) + Cl^-\ (g)$$

Use the following enthalpy changes.

$RbCl\ (s)$	$\rightarrow$	$Rb^+\ (aq)$	$+ \quad Cl^-\ (aq)$	$+17$ kJ mol^{-1}
$Rb^+\ (g)$	$\rightarrow$	$Rb^+\ (aq)$		-301 kJ mol^{-1}
$Cl^-\ (g)$	$\rightarrow$	$Cl^-\ (aq)$		-364 kJ mol^{-1}

Method 1

Step 1 Write the balanced target equation (for the reaction the enthalpy change of which is to be found).

$$RbCl\ (s) \rightarrow Rb^+\ (g) + Cl^-\ (g) \qquad \Delta H\ =\ ?$$

Step 2 Write the balanced equations for the reactions with given enthalpy changes and label them ΔH_a, ΔH_b, etc.

$RbCl\ (s)$	$\rightarrow$	$Rb^+\ (g)$	$+ \quad Cl^-\ (aq)$	ΔH_a
$Rb^+\ (g)$	$\rightarrow$	$Rb^+\ (aq)$		ΔH_b
$Cl^-\ (g)$	$\rightarrow$	$Cl^-\ (aq)$		ΔH_c

Step 3 Identify a second route for the reaction and label each step with the appropriate ΔH value, taking into account
(i)   the number of moles involved,
and
(ii)   the direction of the reaction.

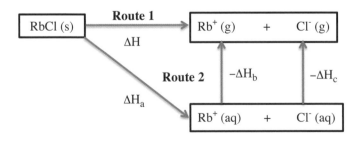

ΔH_b takes a negative sign since the reaction is reversed.
$$Rb^+\ (aq) \rightarrow Rb^+\ (g) \quad = \quad -(-301)\ \text{kJ mol}^{-1}$$
$$= \quad 301\ \text{kJ mol}^{-1}$$

Similarly for ΔHc.

Step 4 Apply Hess's Law.

The enthalpy change for the direct route, i.e. Route 1, will equal the total enthalpy change for Route 2.

$$\Delta H \quad = \quad \Delta H_a \quad + \quad (-\Delta H_b) \quad + \quad (-\Delta H_c)$$

Step 5 Substitute numerical values in the above equation and solve for ΔH.

$$\Delta H \quad = \quad +17 \quad + \quad (+301) \quad + \quad (+364)$$

$$\Delta H \quad = \quad +682 \text{ kJ mol}^{-1}$$

i.e. $RbCl\,(s) \quad \rightarrow \quad Rb^+\,(g) \quad + \quad Cl^-\,(g) \quad \Delta H \quad = \quad \textbf{+682 kJ mol}^{-1}$

Method 2

Write the balanced target equation.

$$RbCl\ (s) \quad \rightarrow \quad Rb^+\ (g) \quad + \quad Cl^-\ (g)$$

Identify a reactant that occurs in this equation.
Use the equation that is given and write down the ΔH value, ΔH_a.

$$\boxed{RbCl\ (s)} \quad \rightarrow \quad Rb^+\ (g) \quad + \quad Cl^-\ (aq) \qquad \Delta H_a = +17\ kJ\ mol^{-1}$$

Identify a product that occurs in this equation, $Rb^+\ (g)$.
Use the equation that is given and write down the ΔH value, ΔH_b.

$$Rb^+\ (g) \quad \rightarrow \quad Rb^+\ (aq) \qquad\qquad \Delta H_b = -301\ kJ\ mol^{-1}$$

Reverse the equation to get the product on the right hand side.
The sign of ΔH_b has to be reversed.

$$Rb^+\ (aq) \quad \rightarrow \quad \boxed{Rb^+\ (g)} \qquad\qquad \Delta H_b = -(-301\ kJ\ mol^{-1})$$
$$= +301\ kJ\ mol^{-1}$$

Identify the second product that occurs in this equation, $Cl^-\ (g)$.
Use the equation that is given and write down the ΔH value, ΔH_c.

$$Cl^-\ (g) \quad \rightarrow \quad Cl^-\ (aq) \qquad\qquad \Delta H_c = -364\ kJ\ mol^{-1}$$

Reverse the equation to get the product on the right hand side.
The sign of ΔH_c has to be reversed.

$$Cl^-\ (aq) \quad \rightarrow \quad \boxed{Cl^-\ (g)} \qquad \Delta H_c = -(-364\ kJ\ mol^{-1})$$
$$= +364\ kJ\ mol^{-1})$$

Applying Hess's Law with the numerical values given

$$\Delta H = \quad \Delta H_a \quad + \quad \Delta H_b \quad + \quad \Delta H_c$$
$$+17 \quad + \quad (+301) \quad + \quad (+364)$$
$$\Delta H = \quad +682\ kJ\ mol^{-1}$$

☐ If the target equation requires more than one mole, then multiply the enthalpy change by the number of moles in the equation.

Example 2: Calculate the enthalpy change for the reaction:

$$2C \ (s) \quad + \quad 3H_2 \ (g) \quad \rightarrow \quad C_2H_6 \ (g)$$

Take the enthalpies of combustion of carbon, hydrogen and ethane to be -394 kJ mol^{-1}, -286 kJ mol^{-1} and -1561 kJ mol^{-1} respectively.

Step 1 Write the balanced target equation.

$$2C \ (s) \quad + \quad 3H_2 \ (g) \quad \rightarrow \quad C_2H_6(g) \qquad \Delta H \ = \ ?$$

Step 2 Write a balanced equation for the reactions with given enthalpy changes and label them ΔH_a, ΔH_b, etc.

C(s)	+	O_2 (g)	$\rightarrow$	CO_2 (g)		ΔH_a
H_2 (g)	+	½O_2 (g)	$\rightarrow$	H_2O (l)		ΔH_b
C_2H_6 (g)	+	3½O_2 (g)	$\rightarrow$	$2CO_2$ (g)	+ 3H_2O (l)	ΔH_c

Step 3 Identify a second route for the reaction and label each step with the appropriate ΔH value, taking into account the number of moles involved and the direction of the reaction.

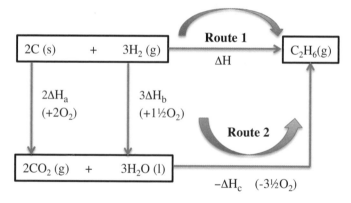

ΔH_a is multiplied by 2 since 2 mol of C(s) are involved.

Likewise, ΔH_b is multiplied by 3.

ΔH_c takes a negative sign since the reaction
$$2CO_2 \ (g) \quad + \quad 3H_2O \ (l) \quad \rightarrow \quad C_2H_6 \ (g) \quad + \quad 3½O_2 \ (g)$$
is the reverse of that for the enthalpy of combustion of ethane.

Step 4 Apply Hess's Law.

The enthalpy change for the direct route, i.e. Route 1, will equal the total enthalpy change for Route 2.

$$\Delta H \quad = \quad 2\Delta H_a \quad + \quad 3\Delta H_b \quad + \quad (-\Delta H_c)$$

Step 5 Substitute numerical values in the above equation and solve for ΔH.

$$\Delta H \quad = \quad 2(-394) \quad + \quad 3(-286) \quad + \quad (+1561)$$

$$\Delta H \quad = \quad \textbf{-85 kJ mol}^{-1}$$

i.e. $2C\,(s) \quad + \quad 3H_2\,(g) \quad \rightarrow \quad C_2H_6\,(g) \quad \textbf{ΔH = -85 kJ mol}^{-1}$

Method 2

Step 1 Write the balanced target equation.

$$2C \text{ (s)} \quad + \quad 3H_2 \text{ (g)} \quad \rightarrow \quad C_2H_6 \text{ (g)}$$

Step 2 Write balanced equations for the given reactions and also write down the ΔH values.

$$2C \text{ (s)} \quad + \quad 2O_2 \text{ (g)} \quad \rightarrow \quad 2CO_2 \text{ (g)} \qquad \Delta H_a \;=\; -394 \text{ kJ mol}^{-1}$$
$$3H_2 \text{ (g)} \quad + \quad 1\tfrac{1}{2}O_2 \text{ (g)} \quad \rightarrow \quad 3H_2O \text{ (l)} \qquad \Delta H_b \;=\; -286 \text{ kJ mol}^{-1}$$
$$C_2H_6 \text{ (g)} \quad + \quad 3\tfrac{1}{2}O_2 \text{ (g)} \rightarrow \quad 2CO_2 \text{ (g)} \;+\; 3H_2O \text{ (l)}$$
$$\Delta H_c \;=\; -1561 \text{ kJ mol}^{-1}$$

Step 3 Identify a reactant that occurs in this equation, C (s).
Use the equation that is given, making sure that the ΔH value corresponds to the number of moles and direction in the target equation.

$$\boxed{2C \text{ (s)}} \quad + \quad 2O_2 \text{ (g)} \quad \rightarrow \quad 2CO_2 \text{ (g)} \qquad \mathbf{2\,\Delta H_a} = 2 \times -394$$
$$= -788 \text{ kJ mol}^{-1}$$

Identify the second reactant that occurs in this equation, H_2 (g).
Use the equation that is given, making sure that the ΔH value corresponds to the number of moles and direction in the target equation.

$$\boxed{3H_2 \text{ (g)}} \quad + \quad 1\tfrac{1}{2}O_2 \text{ (g)} \quad \rightarrow \quad 3H_2O \text{ (l)} \qquad \mathbf{3\,\Delta H_b} = 3 \times -286$$
$$= -858 \text{ kJ mol}^{-1}$$

Identify the product that occurs in this equation, C_2H_6 (g).

Reverse the equation to have the product on the right hand side.
The sign of ΔH_c has to be reversed.

$$2CO_2 \text{ (g)} + 3H_2O \text{ (l)} \quad \rightarrow \quad \boxed{C_2H_6 \text{ (g)}} + \quad 3\tfrac{1}{2}O_2 \text{ (g)}$$
$$\mathbf{\Delta H_c} = -(-1561 \text{ kJ mol}^{-1})$$
$$= 1561 \text{ kJ mol}^{-1}$$

Applying Hess's Law with the numerical values given

ΔH	=	$\mathbf{2\Delta H_a}$	+	$\mathbf{3\Delta H_b}$	+	$\mathbf{\Delta H_c}$
		-788	+	(-858)	+	1561

$$\Delta H \;=\; \mathbf{-85 \text{ kJ mol}^{-1}}$$

Bond enthalpies

☐ For a diatomic molecule, the **molar bond enthalpy** is the energy required to break one mole of bonds. It is also the energy released when one mole of bonds are formed from the gaseous atoms.

☐ Since energy is required to break the X-X or X-Y bonds the reaction is endothermic and the sign of ΔH will be positive.

☐ When covalent bonds are being made the reverse reaction is exothermic and the sign of ΔH will be negative.

Example: The Cl-Cl bond enthalpy is 243 kJ mol⁻¹

$$Cl_2\,(g) \quad \rightarrow \quad 2Cl\,(g) \qquad \Delta H \quad +243 \text{ kJ mol}^{-1}$$

$$2Cl\,(g) \quad \rightarrow \quad Cl_2\,(g) \qquad \Delta H \quad -243 \text{ kJ mol}^{-1}$$

Mean bond enthalpies

☐ The strength of the covalent bond between two different atoms varies slightly from one compound to the next.

☐ The **mean molar bond enthalpy** is the "average" energy required / released in breaking / forming one mole of bonds,

   e.g. *the mean molar bond enthalpy of the C-Cl bond is 338 kJ mol⁻¹.*

☐ Since mean molar bond enthalpies, i.e. average values, are used, enthalpy changes calculated in this way are estimates rather than true values.

☐ Selected molar bond enthalpies and mean bond enthalpies are shown on page 10 of the Data Booklet.

☐ Bond enthalpies can be used to calculate the enthalpy change for a reaction. This is done by calculating the energy required to break bonds in the reactants and the energy released when new bonds are formed in the products.

Example 1: **Use the bond enthalpy values quoted in the Data Booklet to calculate the enthalpy change for the reaction of hydrogen with bromine.**

Step 1   Write the balanced equation for the reaction (sometimes given).

$$H_2 (g) \quad + \quad Br_2 (g) \quad \rightarrow \quad 2HBr (g)$$

Step 2   Draw full structural formula for each of the reactants and products.

H–H   Br–Br   H–Br

Step 3   Identify the bonds broken and the bonds made and list with the corresponding ΔH values.

Bond breaking in kJ mol^{-1}   **Bond making in kJ mol^{-1}**

1 mol H–H   = 436   2 mol H–Br = 2×366 = 732
1 mol Br–Br = 194

Total energy in = +630 kJ   Total energy out = –732 kJ

The + sign is used in bond breaking since such processes are endothermic; the - sign is used in bond making since such processes are exothermic.

Step 4   Complete calculation.

$$\Delta H \quad = \quad +630 \ -732$$

$$= \quad \textbf{–102 kJ mol}^{-1}$$

Example 2: Use the bond enthalpy values quoted in the Data Booklet to calculate the enthalpy change for the reaction of but-2-ene with hydrogen chloride.

Step 1   Write the balanced equation for the reaction (sometimes given).

$$C_4H_8 \text{ (g)} \quad + \quad HCl \text{ (g)} \quad \rightarrow \quad C_4H_9Cl \text{ (g)}$$

Step 2   Draw full structural formula for each of the reactants and products.

```
    H  H  H  H                              H  H  H  H
    |  |  |  |                              |  |  |  |
 H-C -C =C -C -H        H-Cl     →       H -C -C -C -C -H
    |        |                              |  |  |  |
    H        H                              H  H  Cl H
```

Step 3   Identify all the bond breaking and all the bond making and list with the corresponding ΔH values.

Bond breaking in kJ mol^{-1}

1 mol C=C = 612

2 mol C–C = 2×348 = 696

8 mol C–H = 8×412 = 3296

1 mol H–Cl = 432

Total energy in = +5036 kJ

Bond making in kJ mol^{-1}

3 mol C–C = 3×348 = 1044

9 mol C–H = 9×412 = 3708

1 mol C–Cl = 1×338 = 338

Total energy out = –5090 kJ

Step 4   Complete calculation.

$$\Delta H \quad = \quad 5036 -5090 \quad = \quad -54 \text{ kJ mol}^{-1}$$

☐   The calculation can be completed by considering only the bonds broken and the bonds made.

Bond breaking in kJ mol^{-1}

1 mol C=C = 612

1 mol H–Cl = 432
‾‾‾‾‾‾‾‾
          1044

Bond making in kJ mol^{-1}

1 mol C–C = 348

1 mol C–H = 412

1 mol C–Cl = 338
‾‾‾‾‾
          1098

$$\Delta H \quad = \quad 1044 - 1098 \quad = \quad -54 \text{ kJ mol}^{-1}$$

6. REDOX REACTIONS

Oxidation and reduction

☐ **O**xidation **I**s the **L**oss of electrons by a reactant;
Reduction **I**s the **G**ain of electrons by a reactant.

O
I
L **R**
    I
    G

☐ A metal element reacting to form a compound is an example
of oxidation;
a compound reacting to form a metal element is an example
of reduction.

Example 1:   *In the reaction of magnesium with copper(II) sulphate solution, the magnesium atoms lose electrons to form magnesium ions and the copper(II) ions gain electrons to form copper atoms.*

The ion-electron equations for this reaction are:

$Mg(s)$ → $Mg^{2+}(aq)$ + $2e^-$ **oxidation**

$Cu^{2+}(aq)$ + $2e^-$ → $Cu^{2+}(aq)$ **reduction**

Example 2:   *In the reaction of chlorine gas with potassium iodide solution, the chlorine atoms gain electrons to form chloride ions and the iodide ions lose electrons to form iodine.*

The ion-electron equations for this reaction are:

$2I^-(aq)$ → $I_2(aq)$ + $2e^-$ **oxidation**

$Cl_2(g)$ + $2e^-$ → $2Cl^-(aq)$ **reduction**

☐ Oxidation cannot occur without reduction, and vice versa.

☐ Ion-electron equations for reduction reactions can be found on page 12 of the Data Booklet.

☐ To obtain ion-electron equations for oxidation reactions, the equations in the Data Booklet must be turned round.

Writing ion-electron equations

☐ Ion-electron equations for reactions not included in the Data Booklet can be written from first principles.

Example: **Write the ion-electron equation for the reduction of dichromate ions to chromium(III) ions.**

1. Write the formula for the reactant and product.

$$Cr_2O_7^{2-} (aq) \quad \rightarrow \quad Cr^{3+} (aq)$$

2. Balance the chromium.

$$Cr_2O_7^{2-} (aq) \quad \rightarrow \quad 2Cr^{3+} (aq)$$

3. Balance the oxygen by introducing the oxygen needed as water molecules. 7 mol of water will be needed on the RHS of the equation.

$$Cr_2O_7^{2-} (aq) \quad \rightarrow \quad 2Cr^{3+} (aq) \quad + \quad 7H_2O$$

4. Balance the hydrogen by introducing the hydrogen needed as hydrogen ions. 14 mol of $H^+ (aq)$ ions will be needed on the LHS of the equation.

$$Cr_2O_7^{2-} (aq) \ + \ 14H^+ (aq) \quad \rightarrow \quad 2Cr^{3+} (aq) \quad + \quad 7H_2O$$

5. The electrical charge on each side of the equation must be balanced.

The net charge on the LHS of the equation is 12+.

$$Cr_2O_7^{2-} (aq) \quad + \quad 14H^+ (aq)$$
$$(2-) \quad \quad + \quad \quad (14+)$$

The net charge on the RHS of the equation is 6+.

$$2Cr^{3+} (aq) \quad + \quad 7H_2O$$
$$2 \times (3+) \quad + \quad 0$$

Balance the charge by adding moles of electrons to the side which is more positive. 6 mol of electrons will be needed on the LHS of the equation.

$$Cr_2O_7^{2-} (aq) \ + \ 14H^+ (aq) \ + \ 6e- \ \rightarrow \ 2Cr^{3+} (aq) \ + \ 7H_2O$$

☐ Redox reactions of this kind only take place in acidic solution.
The $H^+ (aq)$ ions are needed as a reactant.

Redox reactions

☐ Redox reactions involve the transfer of electrons from one atom, molecule or ion to another.

☐ To form the overall redox reaction, the ion-electron equations for the oxidation and reduction must be combined, ensuring that the number of electrons in the oxidation step cancels out with the number of electrons in the reduction step.

Example 1:   The reaction of magnesium with copper(II) sulphate solution

oxidation $Mg\,(s)$ → $Mg^{2+}\,(aq)$ +   **2e⁻**

reduction $Cu^{2+}\,(aq)$ +   **2e⁻**   → $Cu\,(s)$

---

redox reaction $Mg(s)$ + $Cu^{2+}\,(aq)$ → $Mg^{2+}\,(aq)$ + $Cu\,(s)$

Example 2:   The reaction of aluminium with dilute hydrochloric acid

oxidation $Al\,(s)$ → $Al^{3+}\,(aq)$ +   **3e⁻**

reduction $2H^{+}\,(aq)$ +   **2e⁻**   → $H_2\,(g)$

To balance out the electrons, the oxidation must be multiplied by 2, and the reduction by 3.

oxidation $2Al\,(s)$ → $2Al^{3+}\,(aq)$ +   **6e⁻**

reduction $6H^{+}\,(aq)$ +   **6e⁻**   → $3H_2\,(g)$

---

redox reaction $2Al\,(s)$ + $6H^{+}\,(aq)$ → $2Al^{3+}\,(aq)$ + $3H_2\,(g)$

Oxidising and reducing agents

☐ An **oxidising agent** is a substance that accepts electrons; an oxidising agent brings about oxidation and is reduced in a redox reaction.

☐ A **reducing agent** is a substance that donates electrons; a reducing agent brings about reduction and is oxidised in a redox reaction.

☐ Oxidising and reducing agents can be identified in redox reactions.

Elements

Example 1:   The reaction of zinc with silver nitrate solution

redox reaction $\quad Zn(s) + 2Ag^+(aq) \rightarrow Zn^{2+}(aq) + 2Ag(s)$

oxidation $\quad Zn(s) \rightarrow Zn^{2+}(aq) + 2e^-$

reduction $\quad Ag^+(aq) + e^- \rightarrow Ag(s)$

The Zn (s) atoms lose electrons to form Zn^{2+} (aq) ions and so the Zn (s) atom is the reducing agent. The Ag^+ (aq) ions gain electrons to form to Ag (s) and so the Ag^+ (aq) ion is the oxidising agent.

Example 2:   The reaction of chlorine with sodium iodide solution

redox reaction $\quad Cl_2(g) + 2I^-(aq) \rightarrow 2Cl^-(aq) + I_2 (aq)$

oxidation $\quad 2I^-(aq) \rightarrow I_2(aq) + 2e^-$

reduction $\quad Cl_2(g) + 2e^- \rightarrow 2Cl^-(aq)$

The I^- (aq) ions are oxidised to I_2 (aq) molecules and so I^- (aq) ion is the reducing agent. The Cl_2 (g) molecules are reduced to Cl^- (aq) ions and so the Cl_2 (g) molecule is the oxidising agent.

- [ ] The elements with low electronegativity values (metals) tend to form ions by losing electrons (oxidation) and so can act as reducing agents. The elements with high electronegativity values (non metals) tend to form ions by gaining electrons (reduction) and so can act as oxidising agents.

- [ ] The strongest reducing agents are found in Group 1 whilst the strongest oxidising agents come from Group 7.

- [ ] Metal elements at the top right of the electrochemical series are the strongest reducing agents. Molecules and ions at the bottom left of the electrochemical series are the strongest oxidising agents.

- [ ] Displacement reactions are a good way to compare the relative strength of oxidising and reducing agents.

Molecules and group ions

Example 1: In the reaction of hydrogen peroxide, H_2O_2, with iron(II) ions in acidic solution, the hydrogen peroxide acts as an oxidising agent; the iron(II) ions are oxidised to iron(III) ions.

redox reaction

$$H_2O_2 (aq) + 2Fe^{2+} (aq) + 2H^+ (aq) \rightarrow 2Fe^{3+} (aq) + 2H_2O$$

_____

oxidation $\quad Fe^{2+} (aq) \qquad\qquad\qquad \rightarrow Fe^{3+} (aq) + e^-$

reduction $\quad H_2O_2 (aq) + 2H^+ (aq) + 2e^- \rightarrow 2H_2O (l)$

Example 2: In the reaction of carbon monoxide gas with copper(II) oxide, carbon monoxide acts as a reducing agent; the copper(II) ions are reduced to copper.

redox reaction $\quad CO (g) + CuO (s) \rightarrow Cu (s) + CO_2 (g)$

_____

oxidation $\quad CO (g) + O^{2-} (s) \rightarrow CO_2 (g) + 2e^-$

reduction $\quad Cu^{2+} (s) + 2e^- \rightarrow Cu (s)$

☐ Dichromate and permanganate ions are strong oxidising agents in acidic solutions. The hydrogen ions, H^+ (aq), are needed as one of the reactants.

Example 3: *In the reaction of dichromate ions with iodide ions in acidic solution, the dichromate ion acts as an oxidising agent; the iodide ions are oxidised to iodine molecules.*

redox reaction

$$Cr_2O_7^{2-} (aq) \ + \ 6I^- (aq) \ + \ 14H^+ (aq) \ \rightarrow \ 2Cr^{3+} (aq) \ + \ 3I_2 (aq) \ + \ 7H_2O \ (l)$$

oxidation $2I^- (aq) \qquad\qquad\qquad\qquad \rightarrow \quad I_2 (aq) \ + \ 2e^-$

reduction $Cr_2O_7^{2-} (aq) \ + \ 14H^+ (aq) \ + \ 6e^- \rightarrow \ 2Cr^{3+} (aq) \ + \ 7H_2O \ (l)$

Example 4: *In the reaction of permanganate ions with sulphite ions in acidic solution, the permanganate ion acts as an oxidising agent; the sulphite ions are oxidised to sulphate molecules.*

redox reaction

$$2MnO_4^- (aq) \ + 5SO_3^{2-} (aq) \ + \ 6H^+ (aq) \ \rightarrow 2Mn^{2+} (aq) + 5SO_4^{2-} (aq) + 3H_2O (l)$$

oxidation $SO_3^{2-} (aq) \ + \ H_2O \ (l) \quad \rightarrow \quad SO_4^{2-} (aq) + \ 2H^+ (aq) \ + \ 2e^-$

reduction $MnO_4^- (aq) \ + \ 8H^+ (aq) \ + \ 5e^- \ \rightarrow \ Mn^{2+} (aq) \ + \ 4H_2O \ (l)$

Everyday uses for strong oxidising agents

☐ Oxidising agents are widely employed because of the effectiveness with which they can kill fungi and bacteria and can inactivate viruses.

☐ The oxidation process is also an effective means of breaking down coloured compounds making oxidising agents ideal for use as bleach for clothes and hair,

 e.g. hydrogen peroxide is used to bleach hair.

☐ Potassium permanganate is an oxidising agent that will react with any organic matter in a pond including algae, bacteria, dissolved and bottom sediments. It can be used in fishponds to treat common diseases associated with fish,

 e.g. effect of gill parasites, bacterial and fungal infections.

☐ Bleaching reactions can be carried out using sulphur dioxide,

 e.g. red roses rapidly decolourise in a gas jar of sulphur dioxide.

7. CHEMICAL ANALYSIS

Chromatography

☐ **Chromatography** is a technique that can be used for separating and/or identifying the components of mixtures,

> *e.g. to check the composition and purity of reactants and products in the lab. and as part of the quality control in industrial manufacturing processes; to test for drugs in the urine or blood of athletes and racehorses.*

☐ Separation depends on the mixture being part of a moving phase and being 'dragged' over a non-moving phase. Different compounds 'stick' to the material in the non-moving phase to different extents and so move through/over the material at different speeds.

(a) Gas chromatography

☐ **Gas chromatography** (also known as **gas-liquid chromatography**) involves injecting a liquid sample into a gas stream. The gas carries the mixture in the sample through a column that is packed with a suitable material. The components in the mixture move through the column at different speeds and thus separate out to reach the detector at different times.

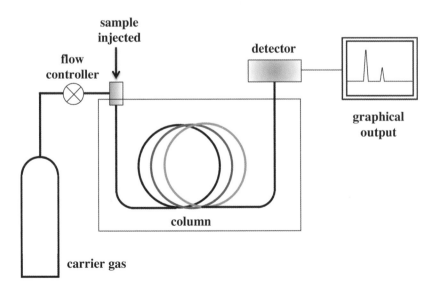

☐ The time taken for each chemical in a mixture to travel through the apparatus and reach the detector is called the **retention time**.

☐ The retention time is related to the mass and polarity of the molecules in the mixture.

☐ Molecules with a higher mass (assuming similar polarity), pass through the column more slowly.

☐ More polar molecules experience greater forces of attraction with the polar molecules in the column and so take longer to pass through the column than non-polar molecules. Molecules with polar groups will have longer retention times than molecules without these groups (assuming similar molecular mass), *e.g. molecules with hydroxyl, carboxyl, carbonyl and amino groups.*

☐ The results of this kind of chromatography can be presented graphically (on a gas chromatogram). A peak showing the retention time is produced on the x-axis when one of the component gases in a mixture is detected. The size of the peak on the y-axis is related to the amount of that component in the mixture.

Example 1: Graph 1 was obtained by injecting a sample containing a mixture of ethane, propane and butane into a gas chromatograph.

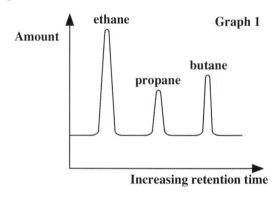

Butane (highest molecular mass) has the longest retention time. The retention time of these molecules is related to their molecular mass since there is no difference in the polarity of the molecules.

Ethane is the most plentiful gas in the mixture while propane is the least plentiful.

Example 2: *Graph 2 was obtained by injecting a sample containing a mixture of methane and ammonia into a gas chromatograph.*

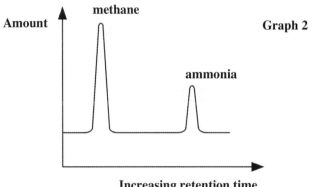

Ammonia (polar) has the longer retention time. The retention time of these molecules is related to their polarity since there is little difference in the mass of the molecules.

Methane is the more plentiful gas in the mixture.

Example 3: *Graph 3 was obtained using three known compounds X, Y and Z; graph 4 was obtained for an unknown compound.*

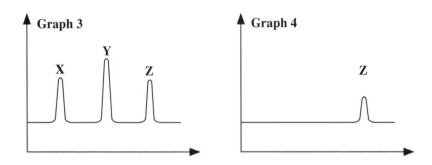

Since the retention time of the unknown is the same as for **Z**, the unknown can be identified as **Z**.

(b) Paper chromatography

☐ **Paper chromatography** involves 'spotting' unknown compounds in a mixture (usually along with known compounds) at a fixed point on to special paper. A suitable solvent is 'soaked up' by the paper, dissolving the compounds which start to travel up the paper with the solvent.

☐ The different compounds move across the paper at different speeds, travelling different distances in the same time. As a result, different compounds in a mixture separate out.

☐ The distance moved by unknown compounds in a mixture can be compared with the distance moved by the known reference compounds. This allows the unknown compounds to be identified.

☐ The distance travelled is related to the mass and polarity of the molecules. The paper is made of a polar material and compounds travel further if they are non-polar. More polar compounds 'bond' with the paper more strongly and therefore do not move so far in the same time.

☐ The distances moved can be compared with the distances moved by known reference compounds. This allows compounds in the mixture to be identified.

Example

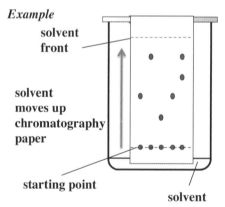

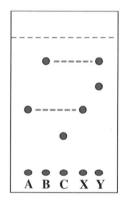

A, B, C are known compounds.
X and Y are unknown compounds.

Since unknown compound **X** in the mixture has moved the same distance as known reference compound **A**, compound **X** must be the same as compound **A**. Unknown compound **Y** is a mixture containing compound **B** and another compound that is neither reference compounds **A** nor **C** .

Volumetric titrations

(a) Neutralisation reactions (revision)

☐ Acids and alkalis react to form a salt plus water in a neutralisation reaction. The concentration of acids and alkalis can be found by **volumetric titrations**.

☐ Neutralisation is complete when all of the H^+ (aq) ions from the acid have been "cancelled out" with exactly the same number of OH^- (aq) ions from the alkali.

$$H^+ \text{ (aq)} \quad + \quad OH^- \text{ (aq)} \quad \longrightarrow \quad H_2O \text{ (l)}$$

☐ The number of moles of H^+ (aq) that react will equal the number of moles of OH^- (aq) that react.

☐ The concentration of acids and alkalis can be found by **volumetric titrations**.

> **Example:** Calculate the volume of sulphuric acid (concentration 0.05 mol l^{-1}) that will neutralise 25 cm^3 of sodium hydroxide solution (concentration 0.2 mol l^{-1}).
>
> $$H_2SO_4 \text{ (aq)} \quad + \quad 2NaOH \text{ (aq)} \quad \rightarrow \quad Na_2SO_4 \text{ (aq)} \quad + \quad 2H_2O \text{ (l)}$$

Step 1	Number of moles of NaOH (aq)	no. of moles	=	conc x litres
			=	0.2 x 0.025
	$\boxed{n = CV}$		=	0.005 mol

Step 2   Use the balanced equation to find the number of moles of H_2SO_4 (aq)

$$2 \text{ mol NaOH (aq)} \leftrightarrow 1 \text{ mol } H_2SO_4 \text{ (aq)}$$
$$0.005 \text{ mol NaOH (aq)} \leftrightarrow 0.0025 \text{ mol } H_2SO_4 \text{ (aq)}$$

Step 3	Calculate the volume of H_2SO_4 (aq)	litres	=	$\dfrac{\text{no. of moles}}{\text{conc}}$
	$\boxed{V = \dfrac{n}{C}}$		=	$\dfrac{0.025}{0.005}$
			=	**0.5 litres (50 cm^3)**

☐ The following relationship can be used to simplify neutralisation calculations.

> vol x conc (mol l^{-1}) x no. of H^+ (aq) in the formula   **ACID**
> = vol x conc (mol l^{-1}) x no. of OH^- (aq) in the formula   **ALKALI**

Example 1:   Calculate the concentration of sodium hydroxide solution, if 25 cm^3 is neutralised by 50 cm^3 of hydrochloric acid (concentration 1 mol l^{-1}).

Step 1   Write relationship   vol x conc x   no. of H^+ (aq)   ACID
                                   = vol x conc x   no. of OH^- (aq)   ALKALI

Step 2a   Number of H^+ (aq) in   HCl (aq) = 1
              formula of acid

Step 2b   Number of OH^- (aq) in   NaOH (aq) = 1
              formula of alkali

Step 3   Put in variables   50 x 1 x 1 = 25 x c x 1

Step 4   Complete calculation   concentration = **2 mol l^{-1}**

Example 2:   Calculate the volume of sulphuric acid (concentration 0.05 mol l^{-1}) that will neutralise 25 cm^3 of potassium hydroxide solution (concentration 0.1 mol l^{-1}).

Step 1   Write relationship   vol x conc x   no. of H^+ (aq)   ACID
                                   = vol x conc x   no. of OH^- (aq)   ALKALI

Step 2a   Number of H^+ (aq) in H_2SO_4 (aq) = 2
              formula of acid

Step 2b   Number of OH^- (aq) in   KOH (aq) = 1
              formula of alkali

Step 3   Put in variables   vol x 0.05 x 2 = 25 x 0.1 x 1

Step 4   Complete calculation   volume = **25 cm^3**

(b) Redox reactions

☐ The procedure used in neutralisation reactions can be applied to redox reactions, i.e. the concentration of a reducing or oxidising agent can be found using

 (a) accurate volumes of the reactants,

 (b) the known concentration of the oxidising or reducing agent,

 (c) the balanced redox equation.

Example 1: Iron(II) ions react with dichromate ions in acidic solution. It was found that 21.6 cm^3 of dichromate solution (concentration 0.1 mol l^{-1}), was required to oxidise 25 cm^3 of a solution containing iron(II) ions.

Equations Fe^{2+} (aq) ➔ Fe^{3+} (aq) + e^-

$Cr_2O_7^{2-}$ (aq) + $14H^+$ (aq) + $6e^-$ ➔ $2Cr^{3+}$(aq) + $7H_2O$ (l)

Calculate the concentration of the iron(II) ion solution.

Step 1   Number of moles   no. of moles = conc x litres
of $Cr_2O_7^{2-}$ (aq)

$$\boxed{n = CV}$$ = 0.1 x 0.0216

                                                       = 2.16 x 10^{-3} mol

Step 2   Use the redox equation to find the number of moles of Fe^{2+} (aq)

1 mol $Cr_2O_7^{2-}$ (aq)   ↔ 6 mol Fe^{2+} (aq)

2.16 x 10^{-3} mol $Cr_2O_7^{2-}$ (aq) ↔ 6 x 2.16 x 10^{-3} mol Fe^{2+} (aq)

                                       = 1.3 x 10^{-2} mol Fe^{2+} (aq)

Step 3   Calculate the concentration $\dfrac{\text{no. of moles}}{\text{litres}}$
of Fe^{2+} (aq)   conc =

$$\boxed{C = \dfrac{n}{V}}$$ = $\dfrac{1.3 \times 10^{-2}}{0.025}$

                                       =   **0.52 mol l^{-1}**

Example 2: Iodine reacts with vitamin C.

Equation $C_6H_8O_6$ (aq) + I_2 (aq) ➜ $C_6H_6O_6$ (aq) + $2H^+$ (aq) + $2I^-$ (aq)
vitamin C

A standard solution of iodine can be used to determine the mass of vitamin C in a carton containing 500 cm^3 of orange juice.

Separate 50.0 cm^3 samples were measured out and then titrated with a 0.0050 mol l^{-1} solution of iodine.
An average of 21.4 cm^3 of the iodine solution was required for the complete reaction with the vitamin C.

Calculate the mass of vitamin C, in grams, in the 500 cm^3 carton of orange juice.

Step 1   Number of moles   no. of moles   =   conc x litres
of I_2 (aq)

                                                =   0.0050 x 0.0214

$$n = CV$$

                                                =   1.07 x 10^{-4} mol

Step 2   Use the balanced equation to find the number of moles of $C_6H_8O_6$ (aq)

1 mol I_2 (aq)   ⟷   1 mol $C_6H_8O_6$ (aq)

1.07 x 10^{-4} mol I_2 (aq)   ⟷   1.07 x 10^{-4} mol $C_6H_8O_6$ (aq)

Step 3   50 cm^3 sample   ⟶   1.07 x 10^{-4} mol of vitamin C

500 cm^3 carton   ⟶   1.07 x 10^{-3} mol of vitamin C

Step 4   Calculate the mass of one mole   6C   8H   6O
(GFM) of vitamin C, $C_6H_8O_6$.   6 x 12   8 x 1   6 x 16
                                       72   8   96
                                              = 176 g

Step 5   Calculate the mass of vitamin C.

$$m = n \times GFM$$ mass =   no. of moles x GFM

                             =   1.07 x 10^{-3} x 176

                             =   **0.19 g**

☐ As with neutralisation reactions there has to be a way of determining the end-point of the reaction. An indicator is commonly used.

Example 1: **The reaction of iron(II) ions with dichromate ions in acidic solution**

Equations Fe^{2+} (aq)   ➔ Fe^{3+} (aq)   + e^-

$Cr_2O_7^{2-}$ (aq)   + $14H^+$ (aq)   + $6e^-$ ➔ $2Cr^{3+}$(aq)   + $7H_2O$ (l)
orange   **green**

Potassium dichromate(VI) solution turns green as it reacts with the iron(II) ions, and there is no way the colour change can be detected when there is one drop of excess orange solution in a strongly coloured green solution.
An indicator has to be added to detect the end point of the reaction.

Example 2: **Starch is used to detect excess iodine in the oxidation of vitamin C.**

Equations $C_6H_8O_6$ (aq)   ➔ $C_6H_6O_6$ (aq) + $2H^+$ (aq) + $2e^-$

I_2 (aq)   + $2e^-$ ➔ $2I^-$ (aq)

As iodine solution is added to the solution of vitamin C in the reaction flask, the iodine molecules are reduced to iodide ions. When all the vitamin C has been used up, the excess iodine produces a blue colour with starch.

☐ For some redox titrations the end-point can be recognised from a colour change involving one of the reactants.
The reaction is said to be self-indicating.

Example: **The reaction of iron(II) ions with permanganate ions in acidic solution**

Equations Fe^{2+} (aq)   ➔ Fe^{3+} (aq)   + e^-

MnO_4^{2-} (aq)   + $8H^+$ (aq)   + $5e^-$ ➔ Mn^{2+} (aq)   + $4H_2O$ (l)
purple   **colourless**

When potassium permanganate solution (purple) reacts with iron(II) sulphate solution, the permanganate ions are reduced to colourless manganese two-positive ions.
At the end-point all the iron(II) ions have been oxidised and the excess permanganate ions cause the purple colour to remain.

PRACTICAL SKILLS

Making measurements

☐ A **pipette** is used to accurately measure out an exact volume of a liquid, *e.g. 10 cm³ or 25 cm³.*

☐ The correct method to use a pipette is to draw the liquid into the pipette using a pipette filler bulb. Draw the liquid to above the mark and then release liquid until the bottom of the meniscus just touches the mark on the pipette.

meniscus

☐ A **burette** also measures out the volume of a liquid. Unlike a pipette, a burette can be used to accurately measure out variable volumes,

e.g. a 50 cm³ burette can be used to measure out volumes up to 50 cm³ to an accuracy of + or – 0.05 cm³.

☐ As with a pipette, the reading of the volume when using a burette corresponds to the bottom of the meniscus.

☐ **Measuring cylinders** can also be used to measure out variable volumes of liquid.

☐ The most accurate measurement for the volume of a liquid (lowest error in the reading) is obtained using a pipette. Measuring cylinders give the least accurate measurement (highest error in the reading).

☐ There is a greater error in the measurement of small quantities than large quantities,

e.g. using the same balance, there is a greater error in the measurement of 1 g of solid than 100 g of solid; using the same burette, the error in a titration that requires 10 cm³ of solution is greater than the error in a titration that requires 30 cm³ of solution.

Standard solutions

☐ A solution of accurately known concentration is known as a **standard solution**.

☐ The following procedure is followed to make a standard solution.

* Using a small beaker, accurately weigh out the approximate mass of substance required.
* Add water to dissolve the substance, stirring if necessary.
* Pour the solution from the beaker into the volumetric flask.
* Using a wash-bottle, rinse out any remaining drops in the beaker and rinse off any drops on the stirring rod.
* Add water to just below the line in the volumetric flask.
* Use a dropping pipette to add the final drops of water until the bottom of the meniscus is on the mark of the flask.

☐ The solid used to make a standard solution must be pure.

☐ Some solids combine with water (from moisture in the air).
Solids used to make a standard solution must be kept dry.

☐ Standard solutions with a low concentration are prepared by dilution of a solution with a higher concentration. A fixed volume is measured out using a pipette, added to a volumetric flask and made up to the mark. This method is preferred due to the error in making very small measurements.

e.g. a 1 mgl^{-1} solution can be prepared in this way by dilution of a 10 gl^{-1} solution.

Volumetric titrations

☐ Volumetric titrations involve using a standard solution to determine the concentration of another solution.

☐ A fixed volume of one reactant solution is added to the reaction flask using a pipette. The other reactant solution is added to the flask using a burette and the volume of this reactant solution required to complete the reaction is determined using an indicator.

☐ The end-point is the point at which the reaction is just complete when all the reactant in the flask has been used up. The excess reactant from the burette produces a colour change with the indicator.

☐ The first titration is used to find the **rough** volume. With this volume known, the titration can be carefully repeated, adding acid very slowly near the end-point, until the volume used can be reproduced (within an acceptable error).

☐ The actual volume used in the calculation is (usually) the average of the second and third titrations ... the rough volume is ignored.

Example

Rough titration /cm^3	Second titration /cm^3	Third titration /cm^3
25.7	24.5	24.3

The volume used in the calculation is **24.4 cm^3**.

☐ When carrying out a titration, all glassware should be rinsed out with water before use. A pipette should then be rinsed with the liquid that is going into the pipette. A burette should then be rinsed with the liquid that is going into the burette.